Microsoft® Internet Explorer™ 5.0
Brief Edition

INTERACTIVE COMPUTING SERIES

Kenneth C. Laudon
Jim Doughty

with Kenneth Rosenblatt

Azimuth Interactive, Inc.

Boston   Burr Ridge, IL   Dubuque, IA   Madison, WI   New York   San Francisco   St. Louis
Bangkok   Bogotá   Caracas   Lisbon   London   Madrid   Mexico City   Milan   New Delhi   Seoul
Singapore   Sydney   Taipei   Toronto

McGraw-Hill Higher Education ⚛

*A Division of The **McGraw-Hill** Companies*

MICROSOFT INTERNET EXPLORER 5.0 BRIEF EDITION
Copyright © 2000 by The McGraw-Hill Companies, Inc. All rights reserved. Printed in the United States of America. Except as permitted under the United States Copyright Act of 1976, no part of this publication may be reproduced or distributed in any form or by any means, or stored in a data base or retrieval system, without the prior written permission of the publisher.

 This book is printed on recycled, acid-free paper containing 10% postconsumer waste.

1 2 3 4 5 6 7 8 9 0 QPD/QPD 9 0 9 8 7 6 5 4 3 2 1 0 9

ISBN 0-07-234081-9

Vice president/Editor-in-Chief: *Michael W. Junior*
Publisher: *David Kendric Brake*
Sponsoring editor: *Trisha O'Shea*
Associate editors: *Scott M. Hamilton/Steve Schuetz*
Developmental editor: *Erin Riley*
Senior marketing manager: *Jeff Parr*
Project manager: *Carrie Sestak*
Production supervisor: *Michael R. McCormick*
Freelance design coordinator: *Pam Verros*
Cover illustration: *Kip Henrie*
Supplement coordinator: *Matthew Perry*
New media: *Lisa Ramos-Torrescan*
Compositor: *Azimuth Interactive, Inc.*
Typeface: *10/12 Sabon*
Printer: *Quebecor Printing Book Group/Dubuque*

Library of Congress Catalog Card Number: 99-66111

http://www.mhhe.com

Microsoft® Internet Explorer™ 5.0
Brief Edition

INTERACTIVE COMPUTING SERIES

Kenneth C. Laudon
Jim Doughty

with Kenneth Rosenblatt

Azimuth Interactive, Inc.

At **McGraw-Hill Higher Education**, we publish instructional materials targeted at the higher education market. In an effort to expand the tools of higher learning, we publish texts, lab manuals, study guides, testing materials, software, and multimedia products.

At **Irwin/McGraw-Hill** (a division of McGraw-Hill Higher Education), we realize technology will continue to create new mediums for professors and students to manage resources and communicate information with one another. We strive to provide the most flexible and complete teaching and learning tools available and offer solutions to the changing world of teaching and learning.

Irwin/McGraw-Hill is dedicated to providing the tools necessary for today's instructors and students to navigate the world of Information Technology successfully.

Seminar Series - Irwin/McGraw-Hill's Technology Connection seminar series offered across the country every year, demonstrates the latest technology products and encourages collaboration among teaching professionals.

Osborne/McGraw-Hill - A division of the McGraw-Hill Companies known for its best-selling Internet titles *Harley Hahn's Internet & Web Yellow Pages* and the *Internet Complete Reference*, offers an additional resource for certification and has strategic publishing relationships with corporations such as Corel Corporation and America Online. For more information, visit Osborne at www.osborne.com.

Digital Solutions - Irwin/McGraw-Hill is committed to publishing Digital Solutions. Taking your course online doesn't have to be a solitary venture. Nor does it have to be a difficult one. We offer several solutions, which will let you enjoy all the benefits of having course material online. For more information, visit www.mhhe.com/solutions/index.mhtml.

Packaging Options - For more about our discount options, contact your local Irwin/McGraw-Hill Sales representative at 1-800-338-3987, or visit our Web site at www.mhhe.com/it.

Preface

Interactive Computing Series

Goals/Philosophy

The *Interactive Computing Series* provides you with an illustrated interactive environment for learning software skills using Microsoft Office. The Interactive Computing Series is composed of both text and multimedia interactive CD-ROMs. The text and the CD-ROMs are closely coordinated. *It's up to you. You can choose how you want to learn.*

Approach

The *Interactive Computing Series* is the visual interactive way to develop and apply software skills. This skills-based approach coupled with its highly visual, two-page spread design allows the student to focus on a single skill without having to turn the page. A running case study is provided through the text, reinforcing the skills and giving a real-world focus to the learning process.

About the Book

The Interactive Computing Series offers *two levels* of instruction. Each level builds upon the previous level.

Brief lab manual - covers the basics of the application, contains two to four chapters.
Introductory lab manual - includes the material in the Brief textbook plus two to four additional chapters.

Each lesson is organized around **Skills**, **Concepts**, and **Steps (Do It!)**.

Each lesson is divided into a number of Skills. Each **Skill** is first explained at the top of the page.
Each **Concept** is a concise description of why the skill is useful and where it is commonly used.
Each **Step (Do It!)** contains the instructions on how to complete the skill.

About the CD-ROM

The CD-ROM provides a unique interactive environment for students where they learn to use software faster and remember it better. The CD-ROM is organized in a similar approach as the text: The **Skill** is defined, the **Concept** is explained in rich multimedia, and the student performs **Steps (Do It!)** within sections called Interactivities. There are at least 45 Interactivities per CD-ROM. Some of the features of the CD-ROM are:

Simulated Environment - The Interactive Computing CD-ROM places students in a simulated controlled environment where they can practice and perform the skills of the application software.
Interactive Exercises - The student is asked to demonstrate command of a specific software skill. The student's actions are followed by a digital "TeacherWizard" that provides feedback.
SmartQuizzes - Provide performance-based assessment of the student at the end of each lesson.

Using the Book

In the book, each skill is described in a two-page graphical spread (Figure 1). The left side of the two-page spread describes the skill, the concept, and the steps needed to perform the skill. The right side of the spread uses screen shots to show you how the screen should look at key stages.

Figure 1

Skill: Each lesson is divided into a number of specific skills

Concept: A concise description of why the skill is useful and where it is commonly used

Running case: A real-world case ties the skill and the concept to a practical situation

Do It!: Step-by-step directions show you how to use the skill

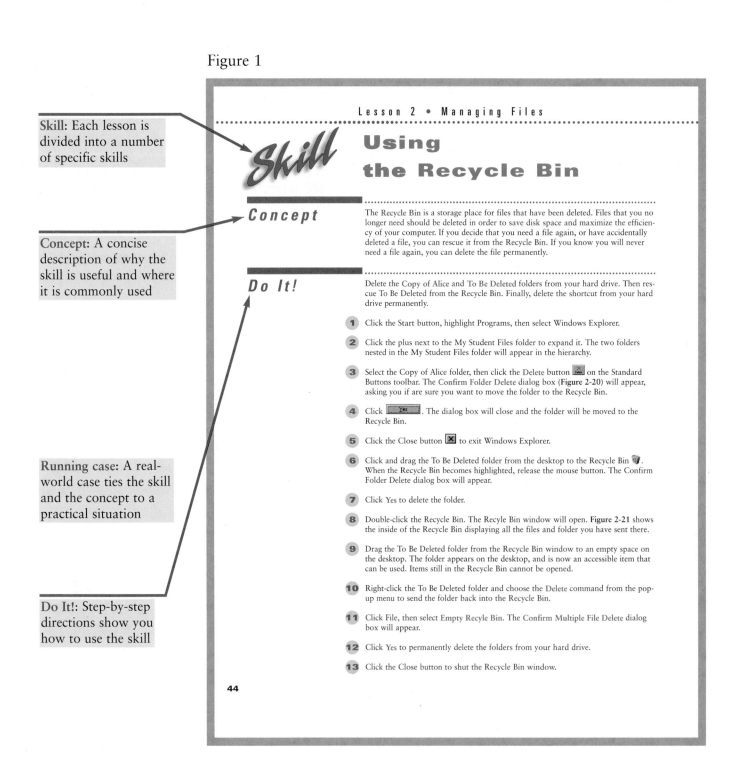

Lesson 2 • Managing Files

Skill

Using the Recycle Bin

Concept

The Recycle Bin is a storage place for files that have been deleted. Files that you no longer need should be deleted in order to save disk space and maximize the efficiency of your computer. If you decide that you need a file again, or have accidentally deleted a file, you can rescue it from the Recycle Bin. If you know you will never need a file again, you can delete the file permanently.

Do It!

Delete the Copy of Alice and To Be Deleted folders from your hard drive. Then rescue To Be Deleted from the Recycle Bin. Finally, delete the shortcut from your hard drive permanently.

1. Click the Start button, highlight Programs, then select Windows Explorer.

2. Click the plus next to the My Student Files folder to expand it. The two folders nested in the My Student Files folder will appear in the hierarchy.

3. Select the Copy of Alice folder, then click the Delete button on the Standard Buttons toolbar. The Confirm Folder Delete dialog box (**Figure 2-20**) will appear, asking you if are sure you want to move the folder to the Recycle Bin.

4. Click **Yes** . The dialog box will close and the folder will be moved to the Recycle Bin.

5. Click the Close button to exit Windows Explorer.

6. Click and drag the To Be Deleted folder from the desktop to the Recycle Bin. When the Recycle Bin becomes highlighted, release the mouse button. The Confirm Folder Delete dialog box will appear.

7. Click Yes to delete the folder.

8. Double-click the Recycle Bin. The Recyle Bin window will open. **Figure 2-21** shows the inside of the Recycle Bin displaying all the files and folder you have sent there.

9. Drag the To Be Deleted folder from the Recycle Bin window to an empty space on the desktop. The folder appears on the desktop, and is now an accessible item that can be used. Items still in the Recycle Bin cannot be opened.

10. Right-click the To Be Deleted folder and choose the Delete command from the pop-up menu to send the folder back into the Recycle Bin.

11. Click File, then select Empty Recycle Bin. The Confirm Multiple File Delete dialog box will appear.

12. Click Yes to permanently delete the folders from your hard drive.

13. Click the Close button to shut the Recycle Bin window.

44

End-of-Lesson Features

In the book, the learning in each lesson is reinforced at the end by a quiz and a skills review called Interactivity, which provides step-by-step exercises and real-world problems for the students to solve independently.

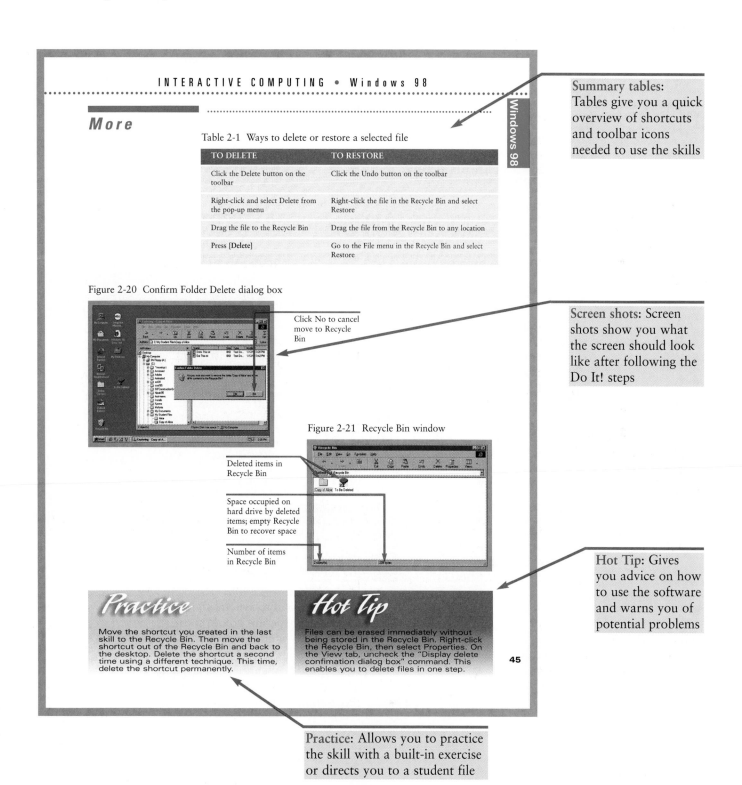

INTERACTIVE COMPUTING • Windows 98

Windows 98

More

Summary tables: Tables give you a quick overview of shortcuts and toolbar icons needed to use the skills

Table 2-1 Ways to delete or restore a selected file

TO DELETE	TO RESTORE
Click the Delete button on the toolbar	Click the Undo button on the toolbar
Right-click and select Delete from the pop-up menu	Right-click the file in the Recycle Bin and select Restore
Drag the file to the Recycle Bin	Drag the file from the Recycle Bin to any location
Press [Delete]	Go to the File menu in the Recycle Bin and select Restore

Figure 2-20 Confirm Folder Delete dialog box

Click No to cancel move to Recycle Bin

Screen shots: Screen shots show you what the screen should look like after following the Do It! steps

Figure 2-21 Recycle Bin window

Deleted items in Recycle Bin

Space occupied on hard drive by deleted items; empty Recycle Bin to recover space

Number of items in Recycle Bin

Hot Tip: Gives you advice on how to use the software and warns you of potential problems

Practice

Move the shortcut you created in the last skill to the Recycle Bin. Then move the shortcut out of the Recycle Bin and back to the desktop. Delete the shortcut a second time using a different technique. This time, delete the shortcut permanently.

Hot Tip

Files can be erased immediately without being stored in the Recycle Bin. Right-click the Recycle Bin, then select Properties. On the View tab, uncheck the "Display delete confimation dialog box" command. This enables you to delete files in one step.

45

Practice: Allows you to practice the skill with a built-in exercise or directs you to a student file

Using the Interactive CD-ROM

The Interactive Computing multimedia CD-ROM provides an unparalleled learning environment in which you can learn software skills faster and better than in books alone. The CD-ROM creates a unique interactive environment in which you can learn to use software faster and remember it better. The CD-ROM uses the same lessons, skills, concepts, and Do It! steps as found in the book, but presents the material using voice, video, animation, and precise simulation of the software you are learning. A typical CD-ROM contents screen shows the major elements of a lesson (see Figure 2 below).

Skills list: A list of skills allows you to jump directly to any skill you want to learn or review, including interactive sessions with the TeacherWizard

Figure 2

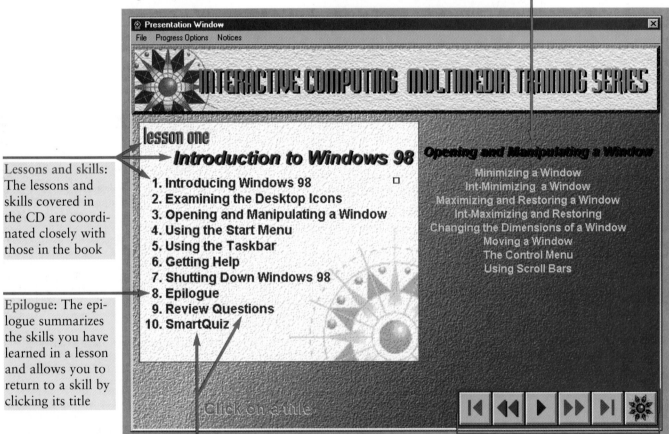

Lessons and skills: The lessons and skills covered in the CD are coordinated closely with those in the book

Epilogue: The epilogue summarizes the skills you have learned in a lesson and allows you to return to a skill by clicking its title

Review Questions and SmartQuiz: Review Questions test your knowledge of the concepts covered in the lesson; SmartQuiz tests your ability to accomplish tasks in a simulated software environment

User controls: Precise and simple user controls permit you to start, stop, pause, jump forward or backward one sentence, or jump forward or backward an entire skill. A single navigation star takes you back to the lesson's table of contents

Unique Features of the CD-ROM: TeacherWizard™ and SmartQuiz™

Interactive Computing: Software Skills offers many leading-edge features on the CD currently found in no other learning product on the market. One such feature is *interactive exercises* in which you are asked to demonstrate your command of a software skill in a precisely simulated software environment. Your actions are followed closely by a digital TeacherWizard that guides you with additional information if you make a mistake. When you complete the action called for by the TeacherWizard correctly, you are congratulated and prompted to continue the lesson. If you make a mistake, the TeacherWizard gently lets you know: "No, that's not the right icon. Click on the Folder icon on the left side of the top toolbar to open a file." No matter how many mistakes you make, the TeacherWizard is there to help you.

Another leading-edge feature is the end-of-lesson SmartQuiz. Unlike the multiple choice and matching questions found in the book quiz, the SmartQuiz puts you in a simulated digital software world and asks you to show your mastery of skills while actually working with the software (Figure 3).

Figure 3

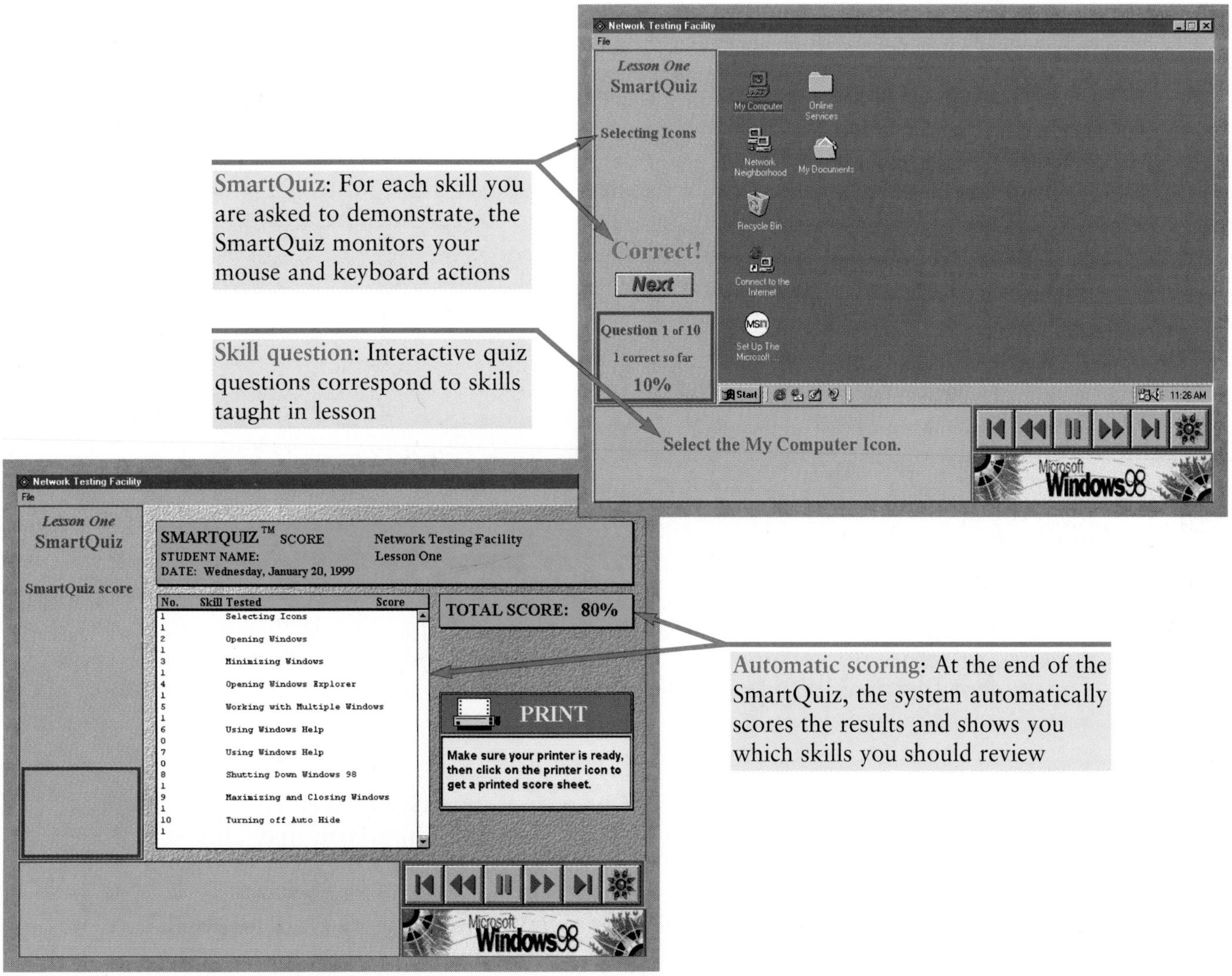

SmartQuiz: For each skill you are asked to demonstrate, the SmartQuiz monitors your mouse and keyboard actions

Skill question: Interactive quiz questions correspond to skills taught in lesson

Automatic scoring: At the end of the SmartQuiz, the system automatically scores the results and shows you which skills you should review

Teaching Resources

The following is a list of supplemental material available with the Interactive Computing Series:

Skills Assessment
Irwin/McGraw-Hill offers two innovative systems, ATLAS and SimNet, which take testing beyond the basics with pre- and post-assessment capabilities.
ATLAS (Active Testing and Learning Assessment Software) – available for the *Interactive Computing Series* – is our live-in-the-application Skills Assessment tool. ATLAS allows students to perform tasks while working live within the Office applications environment. ATLAS is web-enabled and customizable to meet the needs of your course. ATLAS is available for Office 2000.
SimNet (Simulated Network Assessment Product) – available for the *Interactive Computing Series* – permits you to test the actual software skills students learn about the Microsoft Office applications in a simulated environment. SimNet is web-enabled and is available for Office 97 and Office 2000.

Instructor's Resource Kits
The Instructor's Resource Kit provides professors with all of the ancillary material needed to teach a course. Irwin/McGraw-Hill is dedicated to providing instructors with the most effective instruction resources available. Many of these resources are available at our Information Technology Supersite www.mhhe.com/it. Our Instructor's Kits are available on CD-ROM and contain the following:

> Diploma by Brownstone - is the most flexible, powerful, and easy-to-use computerized testing system available in higher education. The diploma system allows professors to create an Exam as a printed version, as a LAN-based Online version, and as an Internet version. Diploma includes grade book features, which automate the entire testing process.
> Instructor's Manual - Includes:
> -Solutions to all lessons and end-of-unit material
> -Teaching Tips
> -Teaching Strategies
> -Additional exercises
> PowerPoint Slides - NEW to the Interactive Computing Series, all of the figures from the application textbooks are available in PowerPoint slides for presentation purposes.
> Student Data Files - To use the Interactive Computing Series, students must have Student Data Files to complete practice and test sessions. The instructor and students using this text in classes are granted the right to post the student files on any network or stand-alone computer, or to distribute the files on individual diskettes. The student files may be downloaded from our IT Supersite at www.mhhe.com/it.
> Series Web Site - Available at www.mhhe.com/cit/apps/laudon.

Digital Solutions
> Pageout Lite - is designed if you're just beginning to explore Web site options. Pageout Lite is great for posting your own material online. You may choose one of three templates, type in your material, and Pageout Lite instantly converts it to HTML.
> Pageout - is our Course Web site Development Center. Pageout offers a Syllabus page, Web site address, Online Learning Center Content, online exercises and quizzes, gradebook, discussion board, an area for students to build their own Web pages, and all the features of Pageout Lite. For more information please visit the Pageout Web site at www.mhla.net/pageout.

OLC/Series Web Sites - Online Learning Centers (OLCs)/Series Sites are accessible through our Supersite at www.mhhe.com/it. Our Online Learning Centers/Series Sites provide pedagogical features and supplements for our titles online. Students can point and click their way to key terms, learning objectives, chapter overviews, PowerPoint slides, exercises, and Web links.

The McGraw-Hill Learning Architecture (MHLA) - is a complete course delivery system. MHLA gives professors ownership in the way digital content is presented to the class through online quizzing, student collaboration, course administration, and content management. For a walk-through of MHLA visit the MHLA Web site at www.mhla.net.

Packaging Options - For more about our discount options, contact your local Irwin/McGraw-Hill Sales representative at 1-800-338-3987 or visit our Web site at www.mhhe.com/it.

Visit www.mhhe.com/it
THE ONLY SITE WITH ALL YOUR CIT AND MIS NEEDS.

Acknowledgments

The Interactive Computing Series is a cooperative effort of many individuals, each contributing to an overall team effort. The Interactive Computing team is composed of instructional designers, writers, multimedia designers, graphic artists, and programmers. Our goal is to provide you and your instructor with the most powerful and enjoyable learning environment using both traditional text and new interactive multimedia techniques. Interactive Computing is tested rigorously in both CD and text formats prior to publication.

Our special thanks to Trisha O'Shea, our Editor for computer applications and concepts, and to Jodi McPherson, Marketing Director for Computer Information Systems. Both Trisha and Jodi have provided exceptional market awareness and understanding, along with enthusiasm and support for the project. They have inspired us all to work closely together. Steven Schuetz provided valuable technical review of our interactive versions, and Charles Pelto contributed superb quality assurance. Thanks to our new Publisher, David Brake, and Mike Junior, Vice-President and Editor-in-Chief. They have given us tremendous encouragement and the needed support to tackle seemingly impossible projects.

The Azimuth team members who contributed to the textbooks and CD-ROM multimedia program are:

Ken Rosenblatt (Textbooks Project Manager and Writer)
Russell Polo (Chief Programmer)
Steven D. Pileggi (Interactive Project Manager)
Jason Eiseman (Technical Writer)
Michael W. Domis (Technical Writer)
Robin Pickering (Developmental Editor, Quality Assurance)
Raymond Wang (Multimedia Designer)
Michele Faranda (Textbook design and layout)
Thomas Grande (Multimedia Designer)
Stefon Westry (Multimedia Designer)
Caroline Kasterine (Multimedia Designer, Writer)
Tahir Khan (Multimedia Designer)
Joseph S. Gina (Multimedia Designer)
Irene A. Caruso (Multimedia Designer)
Josie Torlish (Quality Assurance)

Contents

Internet Explorer 5.0 Brief Edition

Contents

Continued

L E S S O N

1

INTRODUCTION TO THE WORLD WIDE WEB

Perhaps the most popular part of the Internet is the World Wide Web, an enormous array of linked hypertext documents that reside on computers around the world. Its millions of pages contain text, pictures, movies and sounds on almost any topic imaginable. The same resource that brings you NASA's photos from Mars can also deliver movie times, recipes or your nephew's refrigerator drawings. When you switch from viewing one site to viewing another, you may have leapt between host computers thousands of miles apart, but the material is presented to you as if you've merely turned a page. The content of the World Wide Web (often called the WWW, or simply the Web) is limited only by the imaginations of the people who create pages for you to view.

Microsoft Internet Explorer 5 is a software application that gives you the tools you need to take full advantage of the Web. Using it, you will be able to view items for information or entertainment, search for answers to questions, keep in touch with friends and loved ones and even purchase goods and services. Internet Explorer integrates with your Windows 98 operating system to make "browsing" the Web a seamless part of your computing experience. When using Internet Explorer, most Web browsing can be done through a series of mouse clicks. Web pages contain hypermedia – words and pictures that are linked to other sites on the Web and will transport you there when you click on them. Internet Explorer also contains menus and toolbars that help you move through the material on the Web and put it to use. Note that a "site" is an address on the Web that may be made up of one or more pages, but the terms "site" and "page" are often used interchangeably.

In its simplest form, browsing the Web requires only that you type the address of a Web site into a text box on Internet Explorer called the Address Bar. Of course, there are many other ways to access Web sites, and we will visit them all during the skill lessons ahead. You can also save organized lists of your favorite sites, search for sites based upon topics you want to learn about or questions you want to answer, and take data from the Web for your own use. As you read this book, remember that the sites included here as examples may have changed since the authors visited them, and don't be surprised if you see something different when you follow in their footsteps. The ever-changing nature of the Web is one of the things that makes it such a rewarding "place" to visit.

Introducing the Internet

Concept

The Internet is an extended world-wide computer network that is composed of numerous smaller networks. In the late 1960s, the U.S. Department of Defense's Advanced Research Projects Agency (ARPA) created a network of computers designed to withstand severe localized damage, such as that of a nuclear attack. Each computer on the ARPA network was connected to every other machine in such a way as to form a web. Each "chunk" of data sent from one machine to another was formatted as a packet, which also contained the address of where the packet originated and where it was headed. The web configuration and packet format enabled data to be rerouted if a node along its path in the network should be rendered inoperable. The packet-switching technology developed for ARPAnet became the foundation of today's Internet.

In the early 1980s, the National Science Foundation created NSFnet, five supercomputing centers connected together on a network. Soon, other government agencies and educational institutions connected to NSFnet as well, adding information and infrastructure upon which an ever-larger network began to grow.

As more scientists, students, and computer enthusiasts became familiar with the Internet, more people began to log on from a variety of locations, and Internet use grew rapidly. Soon, new software was developed to facilitate access to the Internet. Along with electronic mail and newsgroups, two major uses of the Internet, the World Wide Web began to rise in popularity.

The WWW is made possible by hypermedia and hypertext: objects such as pictures, icons, or lines of text that not only display information but serve as "buttons." When the user mouse-clicks these objects, the computer is instructed to access another location on the Web. This allows for a nonlinear presentation of information, making the WWW, in effect, one huge hypermedia document made up of millions of individual files, each with its own address on the Web. The address at which a document is located on the Internet is called a Uniform Resource Locator or URL. A URL consists of three parts: the protocol, such as http (HyperText Transfer Protocol) or ftp (File Transfer Protocol); the location of the server on the Internet; and sometimes the path to the requested data on the server's drive.

The Web works on a client-server model (see **Figure 1-1**). The server is the computer that contains the requested data. It sends information to the computer that requests it, called the client. The transfer of data between the server and the client follows a standardized protocol, or information exchange process. The Web standard is HTTP, which allows all kinds of computers to understand and reliably translate hypertext Web files. Internet Explorer is a Web browser, which like all Web software conforms to HTTP standards. Web browsers are programs that allow a computer to translate the hypertext and display it. All Web software can read all Web pages because these pages are written with a platform-independent language called HyperText Markup Language, or HTML. HTML documents consist of the text that will appear on the page, formatting instructions, and references to other files such as graphics that will be displayed on the page. The World Wide Web has become the most popular feature of the Internet, providing access to an almost unimaginable diversity of information.

What is Internet Explorer?

Concept

Among other things, Internet Explorer:

1 Allows you to translate and display HTML documents in a readable format.

2 Permits you to save the URLs of Web sites you wish to revisit, and to organize the URLs you've saved – called Favorites – in files you create.

3 Lets you print the content you read on the Web, or save it to a disk.

4 Helps you search the Web when you have a topic, a name or a question, but not the specific URL of the site you need.

5 Lets you interact with certain Web sites by sending information you type back over the Internet.

6 Allows you to exert control over the display of Web materials whose content may be unsuitable for some viewers.

Figure 1-1 Clients and servers on the World Wide Web

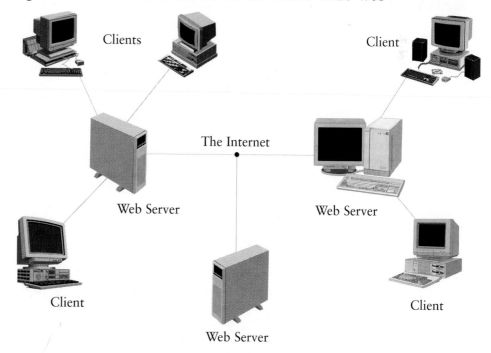

Opening Internet Explorer

Concept

Before you can begin surfing the Web with Internet Explorer (IE), you must open the application. As with many applications, you can do this in a variety of ways including using the Start menu, the Quick Launch toolbar, or a desktop icon.

Do It!

Open Internet Explorer using the Start menu.

1 Click the Start button ![Start] on the Windows taskbar. The Start menu appears.

2 Move the mouse pointer over the Start menu until it is pointing to Programs. The Programs submenu will appear.

3 Move the pointer straight across to the submenu and then down so it is pointing to Internet Explorer as in **Figure 1-2**.

4 Click Internet Explorer. Assuming your connection to the Internet is valid, Internet Explorer will open. If you are using a dial-up service and are not already on-line, a dialog box will appear as in **Figure 1-3** prompting you to establish a connection before you can begin using Internet Explorer.

5 The Internet Explorer browser window (see **Figure 1-4**) will open to a Web site that has been selected as your home page. Later you will learn how to change this setting to a page of your choosing.

More

If you are using Windows 98, try right-clicking your mouse on the menu item for Internet Explorer when it appears on the Start menu. You will be given an option to Create Shortcut. Once you create it, you can drag the shortcut from the Start menu to the Quick Launch toolbar, where it will become a button featuring the Internet Explorer logo. In the future, you will be able to open the program simply by clicking once on that button. An Internet Explorer Quick Launch button may have been created for you when you installed Windows 98.

If you are using Windows 95 or would rather create a desktop shortcut to Internet Explorer, use the Start menu to open Windows Explorer and locate the Internet Explorer program on it. Right-clicking the entry for Internet Explorer will bring up several options including Create Shortcut. The shortcut icon will appear on your operating system's desktop, and in the future you will be able to open the program by double-clicking the icon.

Figure 1-2 Starting Internet Explorer

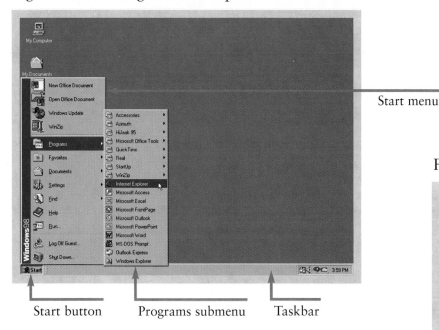

Start menu

Start button   Programs submenu   Taskbar

Figure 1-3 Dialing up

Figure 1-4 Internet Explorer browser window

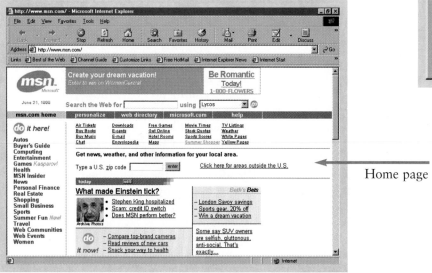

Home page

Hot Tip

Applications running under Windows are represented by program buttons on the taskbar. You can click these buttons to toggle between programs without having to open or close them.

Internet Explorer 5.0

Exploring the Browser Window

Concept

The window in which Internet Explorer displays Web documents is called the browser window (see **Figure 1-5**). It contains several different groups of controls to simplify and organize the way in which you use the program.

Do It!

Guide your pointer over the various parts of the browser window to become familiar with its features.

Near the top of the window, similar to many other applications, is the menu bar (File/Edit/View/Favorites/Tools/Help). Click one of these menu titles to reveal a menu of commands. Slide your pointer to another option on the menu bar to produce a different menu of commands. Clicking any one of these commands will execute it. For now, click again with your pointer at the top of the menu bar to close the open menu.

In the upper-right corner of the window, beyond the menu bar, is an Internet Explorer icon. When this icon is in motion – appearing to spin – it signifies that the program is actively seeking or loading information from the Web. When it is still, the activity has stopped.

Below the menu bar is Internet Explorer's Standard Buttons toolbar (displayed in **Figure 1-6**), which allows you one-click access to some of the program's most commonly used functions. Later in this text you will learn how each of these functions works.

Below the Standard Buttons toolbar is the Address Bar. This is where you type in a Web site's URL to manually access the site. It is also where Internet Explorer automatically displays the URL of the site you are visiting no matter how you got there. Note that the right end of the Address Bar is a button with a down arrow; clicking this button reveals a menu of sites in your History file, or sites you have visited recently. When you begin to use Internet Explorer for the first time, this menu will be blank except for your home page. The Go button to the right of the arrow executes the command to access the URL specified in the Address Bar. Alternately, you can achieve the same effect after entering a URL by typing [Enter].

Between the Address Bar and the display window is the Links toolbar, which contains buttons that you can click to visit specific Web sites. The Links toolbar comes with buttons supplied by Microsoft, but you can add your own favorite sites.

More

On the bottom of the browser window is the browser's status bar. It will tell you when the application is searching for a site, connecting to it, or finished retrieving information. If you have positioned your mouse pointer over a hyperlink, this display will reveal the URL to which the hyperlink is connected even before you click it. In the bottom right-hand corner, the browser window displays the security "zone" in which a page is located. Zones will be explained later.

Figure 1-5 Exploring the browser window

Menu bar

Standard Buttons toolbar

Address Bar

Links toolbar

Status bar

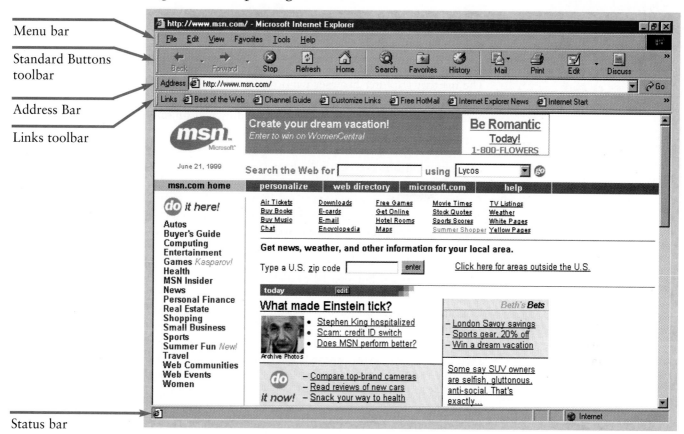

Internet Explorer 5.0

Figure 1-6 Standard Buttons toolbar

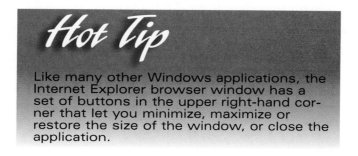

Like many other Windows applications, the Internet Explorer browser window has a set of buttons in the upper right-hand corner that let you minimize, maximize or restore the size of the window, or close the application.

Customizing the Browser Window

Concept

The Internet Explorer browser window can be altered in certain ways to suit your personal preferences. It will still perform the same functions in the same manner, but the location of certain items in the window will simply be rearranged.

Do It!

Customize various aspects of the browser window.

1. To alter the order in which Standard Buttons toolbar buttons are displayed, right-click anywhere on the Standard Buttons toolbar (or select View from the menu bar and position your mouse pointer over Toolbars) and select Customize from the pop-up menu that appears (see **Figure 1-7**). It does not matter which of the buttons you right-click. A dialog box titled Customize Toolbar appears that offers several options. In the scrolling list box labeled Current toolbar buttons, click the Home icon (scroll up if you do not see it). Holding down your mouse button, drag the icon up two spaces on the list. As you drag, a small arrow will appear to show you where the icon will be placed when you release the mouse button (see **Figure 1-8**). Let go of the mouse button when the arrow is between Forward and Stop. The Home button will now appear between Forward and Stop on the toolbar. As an alternate method, you could highlight Home with a single click and then click the Move Up button Move Up until Home appears in the proper place. When you click Close and the Customize Toolbar box closes, you will see that the Standard Buttons toolbar on your browser window reflects the change you have made.

2. If you want to remove a Standard Buttons toolbar button altogether, open the Customize Toolbar box, click the function you want to remove in the Current toolbar buttons list, and then click <-Remove. To add a button from the list of extras on the left, highlight it and click Add ->, or drag the icon from one list to the other.

3. To move the Address Bar, click and hold on the word Address. Your mouse pointer will change to a four-way arrow (see **Figure 1-9**). Drag the Address Bar anywhere you want in relation to the other menus and toolbars: above the menu bar, above the Standard Buttons toolbar, or even to the right of either. When the setup you see appears satisfactory, release your mouse button to drop the menu in its new location. You can move the Standard Buttons and Links toolbars in the same manner.

4. To remove a menu or toolbar entirely, select View from the menu bar and point to the Toolbars command. A list of available items appears. If the item you want to remove has a check mark next to it, click it and it will be deactivated. To restore a menu or toolbar, go to the same list and click its name again.

More

The Customize Toolbar dialog box also allows you to select whether text labels for each of the buttons will be displayed underneath them, to the right, or not at all. It also enables you to select large or small icons. It may be best to use the default settings for a while until you gain familiarity with Internet Explorer and your own use patterns. Rearranging buttons and toolbars should be done to maximize efficiency, not to make the window "look good." Unnecessary changes may decrease your efficiency and cost you more time and effort down the line.

Figure 1-7 Toolbars pop-up menu

Check mark indicates
an active feature

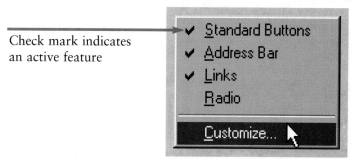

Internet Explorer 5.0

Figure 1-8 Customize Toolbar dialog box

Arrow indicates
where icon will be
dropped when mouse
button is released

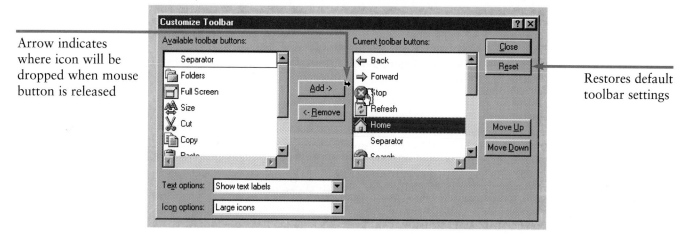

Restores default
toolbar settings

Figure 1-9 Moving the Address Bar

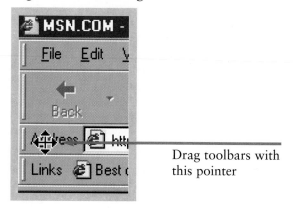

Drag toolbars with
this pointer

Practice

Move the Home button back to its original position.

Hot Tip

Changing the appearance of the browser window is not permanent, so you are free to experiment with arrangements you like without fear of losing anything.

 **Your Home Page**

Concept

When using Internet Explorer, you can select any Web page you wish to view. When you open the application, however, it will go automatically to a certain page. This is called the home page. You can also access your home page at any time by clicking the Home button on the Standard Buttons toolbar. When you first install Internet Explorer, the home page will be set to the Microsoft Network's Web site (http://www.msn.com) as a default. You can change your home page setting easily.

Do It!

Change your browser's home page setting to a different page.

1 Click Tools on the menu bar, then click Internet Options. The Internet Options dialog box (see **Figure 1-10**) opens to the General tab. In the Home page section of the tab, the current home page address is highlighted in the Address: box. To change the home page, simply type a new address.

2 Type http://www.loc.gov, which will be the address of your new home page. To make the Microsoft Network site your home page again, you would merely click the Use Default button | Use Default |. If you wanted Internet Explorer to open to a blank screen each time you start the program, click the Use Blank button | Use Blank |. If you know the URL of a particular page, type it into the text box. If you were browsing a page before opening the Internet Options box and want to make that page your home page from now on, click the Use Current button | Use Current |.

3 Click | OK | at the bottom of the dialog box to confirm the new setting and close the dialog box. The next time you start the program or click [home], the home page of the Library of Congress will be the page your browser displays.

More

Your home page can be any site you choose. If you frequently do research, you may choose an Internet search engine site, a database on a specific topic, or even the Library of Congress Web site as above. If your extended family keeps in touch using a Web page, you may want Internet Explorer to open to that page so you can see news and photos of your loved ones. Many people choose the Web pages of newspapers, news services, or weather information services as their home pages.

Be aware that on Web sites that contain more than one page of material, the "main" page that introduces visitors to the site and contains links to the other pages is also referred to as a "home page." These are two different uses of the same term.

Figure 1-10 Internet Options dialog box

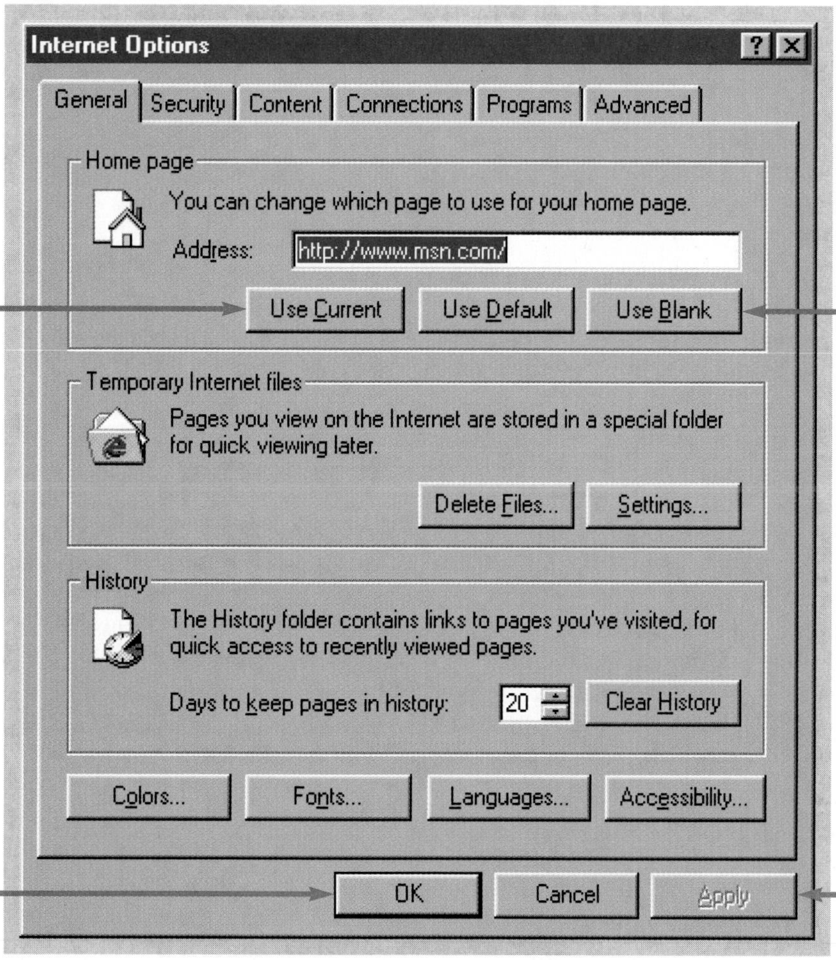

Internet Options

General | Security | Content | Connections | Programs | Advanced

Home page
You can change which page to use for your home page.
Address: http://www.msn.com/

[Use Current] [Use Default] [Use Blank]

Sets page currently loaded in browser as home page

Uses a blank page as home page

Temporary Internet files
Pages you view on the Internet are stored in a special folder for quick viewing later.

[Delete Files...] [Settings...]

History
The History folder contains links to pages you've visited, for quick access to recently viewed pages.

Days to keep pages in history: 20 [Clear History]

[Colors...] [Fonts...] [Languages...] [Accessibility...]

[OK] [Cancel] [Apply]

Click to confirm new settings and return to browser window

Click to apply new settings and keep dialog box open

Practice

Change your home page to the New York Times site, **www.nytimes.com**. Click the Home button to see if you have done it correctly. Then, change your home page back to the default Microsoft site and click the Home button again.

Hot Tip

If you especially like a site and decide to make it your home page, you may also wish to save it as a Favorite, a procedure which you will learn about later. That way, you will still have the URL of the site saved if you change your home page later.

Changing the Way Text is Displayed

Concept

To a certain extent, you can control the way a Web page is displayed through your browser. You can change the size or font of the text, for example, to make it easier to read. You can also change the text color, which can make a big difference in readability depending upon the background color of the page you are viewing.

Do It!

Change the size of the text and the background color of the Web page you are viewing.

1 On the menu bar, click View, and position your mouse pointer over the Text Size command to highlight it. A submenu listing different size options will appear. The bullet on the left side of the submenu marks the current size.

2 Click Largest on the submenu. The text on the page will increase in size, as shown in **Figure 1-11**.

3 Change the text size back to Medium.

4 Click Tools, then click Internet Options to open the Internet Options dialog box.

5 Click the Accessibility button Accessibility.... In the Accessibility dialog box that appears, if the option marked Ignore colors specified on Web pages does not have a checkmark next to it, click the check box to put one there. Click OK at the bottom of the Accessibility dialog box. In the background, you will see the colors of the page in your browser window change.

6 Back in the Internet Options dialog box, click the Colors button Colors.... The Colors dialog box will open.

7 Click the Use Windows colors check box to remove the check mark from it. The Text and Background color buttons will become active.

8 Click the Background color button. The Color dialog box will appear.

9 Click the yellow color square in the second row of the Basic colors palette to select it. Then click OK. The Background color button now displays the color you selected (see **Figure 1-12**).

10 Click OK in the Colors dialog box, and again in the Internet Options dialog box. MSN's home page is shown with its new background color in **Figure 1-13**.

More

You may have noticed that the Colors dialog box has a second set of buttons that are devoted to setting colors for links. Usually, text hyperlinks on Web pages are displayed in different colors from the rest of the text: one color is used to alert the user that a hyperlink is present, and another color is used to indicate that a hyperlink has already been followed (clicked). You can change these colors as well. The option Use hover color sets a third color that will "take over" a hyperlink any time your mouse pointer is positioned over it.

Figure 1-11 Web page with Largest text size

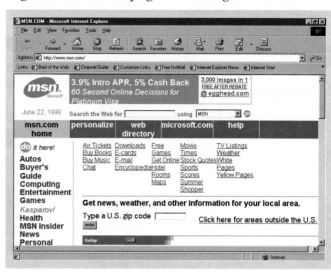

Figure 1-12 Colors dialog box

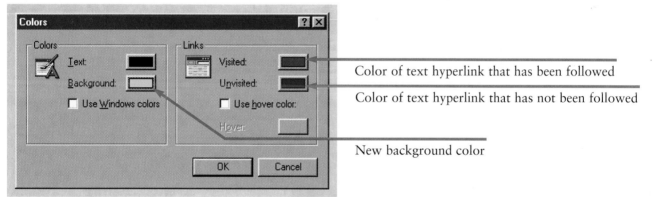

Color of text hyperlink that has been followed

Color of text hyperlink that has not been followed

New background color

Figure 1-13 Page with new background color

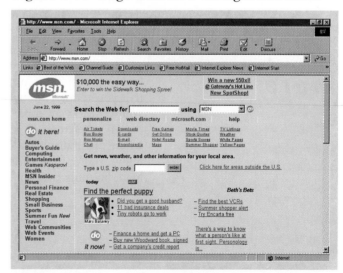

Practice

Change the Web page you are viewing so that it has small green text on a red background. Then restore your browser's color and accessibility settings to their defaults (use Windows colors and colors specified on Web pages).

Hot Tip

Make sure to select colors that provide adequate contrast. If your text color and background color are too similar, text will be very difficult to read. Some colors can also combine in ways that are jarring to the eye.

Controlling the Display of Graphics on a Page

Concept

Web pages are enhanced by the use of pictures along with text. Laying out the graphics in pleasing and useful ways can be a Web designer's whole job. Still, there are times when you wish to see only the text content of a page. This happens most often when your Internet connection is slow or the page is very large, and you want to "cut to the chase" and access the text as quickly as possible.

Do It!

Turn off the display of pictures on a Web page.

1 Click Tools on the menu bar, then click Internet Options.

2 When the Internet Options dialog box opens, look among the tabs at the top and click the one labeled Advanced.

3 Scroll down to the section headed Multimedia and click the check box labeled Show Pictures to remove the check mark from it, as shown in **Figure 1-14**.

4 Click ☐ OK ☐ to close the Internet Options dialog box and confirm the new setting.

5 Click the Refresh button 🔁 on the Standard Buttons toolbar. The current page will be reloaded into your browser, but this time the pictures will not appear (see **Figure 1-15**). As long as you leave the settings the same, all subsequent pages will load without pictures. To restore the original settings, go back to the Advanced tab in the Internet Options dialog box and place a check mark in the Show Pictures check box.

More

Even when pictures are not displayed, the context of a page or a text caption often tells you enough about the available pictures to let decide if you want see them. If you want to view a particular image on a page even though you have turned off the display of pictures in general, you do not have to change your settings. In the space where the undisplayed picture would have been, right-click your mouse and select Show Picture from the pop-up menu that appears. The picture you've selected will load, but only that one.

Figure 1-14 Advanced tab

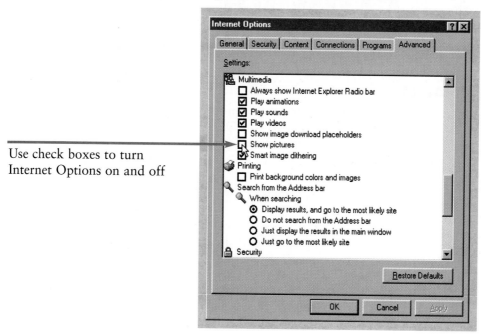

Use check boxes to turn
Internet Options on and off

Figure 1-15 Web page without pictures

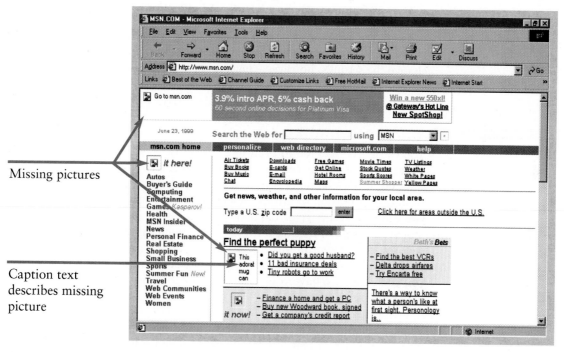

Missing pictures

Caption text
describes missing
picture

Practice

Set your browser to show pictures again if
you have not already reactivated this
option.

Hot Tip

The Advanced tab in the Internet Options
dialog box gives you similar control over
the display of animations, video clips, and
sounds.

Printing Material from the Web

Concept

If you have a printer that is properly connected to your computer, you can print entire Web pages or parts of Web pages. Keeping a hard copy of a Web page is a good idea if you want to save the contents of a Web page that changes frequently.

Do It!

Print the entire contents of a Web page.

1 With the page displayed in the browser window, click File on the menu bar, and then click Print. The Print dialog box, shown in **Figure 1-16**, appears.

2 The Print dialog box provides several options for printing a page. To print the whole Web page, look to the section labeled Print range and make sure the All radio button is selected. Also make sure the printer you wish to use appears in the Name box in the top section of the dialog box. If not, click the drop-down arrow and select the correct printer from the list of available printers that opens.

3 Click OK to print the page.

4 After you have printed a page for the first time this way and verified that the settings are the way you want them, you can do your next printing job merely by clicking the Print button on the Standard Buttons toolbar. Any time you wish to change the settings, however – page range, number of copies, or any other parameter – you will have to return to the Print dialog box via the File menu to make the changes.

More

You can select material to print in a variety of ways. For example, many Web pages are actually several pages long (a "page" in a Web document does not always correspond to one computer screen or one piece of letter-size paper), and you may want only a portion of it to print. In the Print range section of the Print dialog box, you can specify a page or range of pages to print. Another option is to use your mouse to highlight text on the Web page, much as you would with a word processor. You can then print only the text you want by clicking the Selection radio button in the Print range area. In the section of the Print dialog box labeled Copies, you can choose to have your printer automatically print more than one copy of the material you've selected.

Some Web pages are presented in a format called frames, which divides the page into different areas that scroll and change independently from each other. If the page you are printing uses frames, a segment of the Print dialog box labeled Print frames will become active (see **Figure 1-17**), giving you the chance to decide what will be printed: all the frames as they appear on the screen, all the frames one after the other, or only the selected frame. The selected frame is the one in which you last clicked your mouse or performed an operation.

If you have a color printer, you may wish to turn off color printing when you just want a quick copy of a Web page's contents. Color printing is slower and more costly. Click the Properties button in the Print dialog box; the menu you produce will differ depending on what printer you have, but most color printers will offer a simple option such as Print in Grayscale or Black and White.

Figure 1-16 Print dialog box

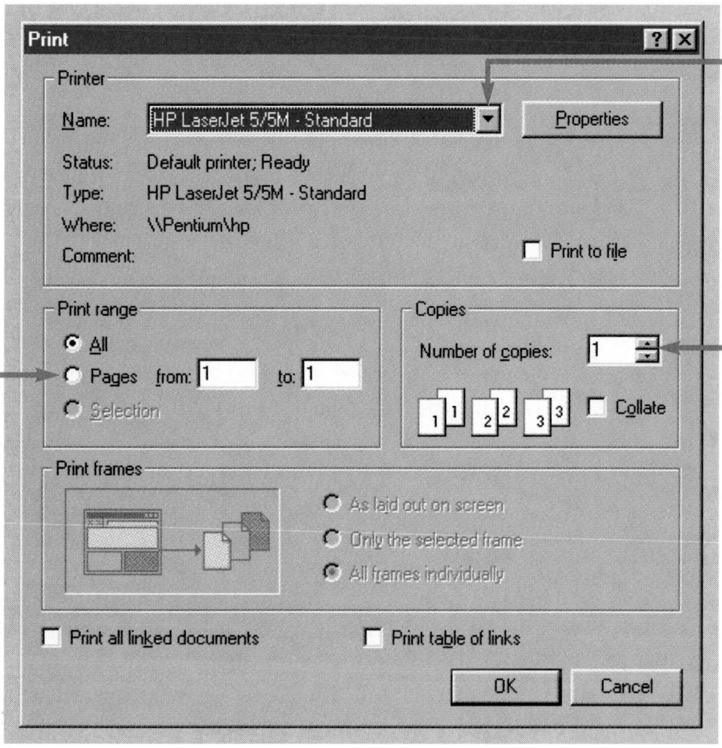

Click to select a different printer

Click to specify a page or range of pages to be printed

Click arrows to change number of copies to be printed

Figure 1-17 Printing frames

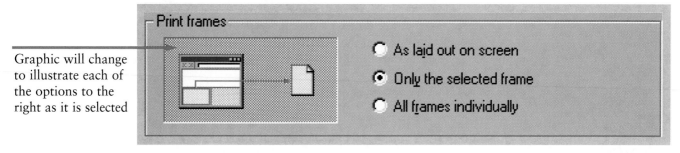

Graphic will change to illustrate each of the options to the right as it is selected

Practice

Print out only one paper page of the Web page you are currently viewing. Then, highlight a paragraph of text and print only that.

Hot Tip

The **Collate** option in the Print dialog box allows you to print a full set of document pages in order before starting the next set when you are printing more than one copy of a multiple page document.

Saving a Web Page

Concept

When you view a Web page, its contents are loaded from the Internet into your computer's memory, but that part of the computer's memory is temporary and may be erased when it becomes full or when you turn off your computer. You may wish to save a Web page onto a disk so you can view it later or send its contents to someone else via e-mail.

Do It!

Save a Web page into a folder on your computer's hard drive.

1. With the page you wish to save displayed on the screen, click File and then click Save As (see **Figure 1-18**). The Save Web Page dialog box appears.

2. The Save in: drop-down list box allows you to choose where the Web page will be saved. The default location is the My Documents folder on your hard drive. If you want to select a different storage location, click the arrow at the of the box. A list of all the top level locations available to you will appear. If you click one of these locations, its contents will appear in the window below the Save in: box. To select a lower level folder as your Save in: location, double-click it in the contents window.

3. Once the name of the folder you want appears in the Save in: box, click the arrow at the right of the box labeled Save as type:. Four options appear:

   •Web Page, complete will save everything on the page, including text, pictures, hyperlinks and the layout in which they were presented on the Web.
   •Web Archive for email will save a snapshot of the current Web page so that it can be displayed or e-mailed as a single file later.
   •Web Page, HTML only will save the HyperText Markup Language information on the Web page, but not the pictures or other files to which the HTML refers.
   •Text File will save the text content of the page and nothing else.

4. Click the first option, Web Page, complete, which was the default option.

5. The default file name for a Web page is the name that the page's author assigned to appear in the browser window's title bar. Click and drag over this name to highlight it in the File name: box, and replace it with Doit1-10. Your Save Web Page dialog box should look similar to **Figure 1-19**.

6. Once the file name, file type, and destination folder are displayed as you want them, click ▐ Save ▐. The page will be saved to your hard drive.

More

Remember that when you call up the pages you have saved later on, they are coming from your disk drive, not from the Internet. Pages whose contents change frequently, such as news and weather sites, will not be updated. Unless you have saved a page in its complete format and are connected to the Internet when you retrieve it for view, the hyperlinks contained in it will not be active.

Internet Explorer automatically saves the contents of pages you've viewed recently in a location called Temporary Internet Files, mainly for the purpose of reloading them more quickly when you return to them. The Save functions described above give you a greater range of options, however, in how you save Web materials and how you use what you've saved.

Figure 1-18 Using the Save As command

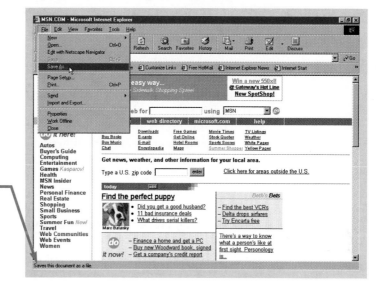

Description of highlighted command appears in status bar

Figure 1-19 Save Web Page dialog box

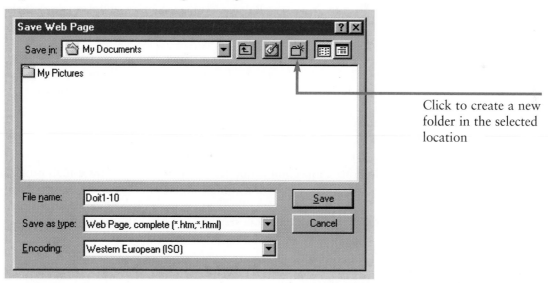

Click to create a new folder in the selected location

Practice

Save the page you are viewing to your desktop under the name **Prac1-10**.

Hot Tip

If you are in the habit of saving files from the Web, you may want to create a folder especially for that purpose. That way you will avoid cluttering the My Documents folder, which is also the default folder for saved files from many other applications.

Activating an E-mail Program from Your Browser

Concept

For most people, the Internet connection through which Web pages arrive is the same one used for e-mail messages. Internet Explorer does not handle e-mail itself, but it is designed to work with other programs that do, such a Microsoft Outlook.

Do It!

Select an e-mail program to access from Internet Explorer.

1 From the menu bar, select Tools and click Internet Options.

2 Click the Programs tab to bring it to the front of the dialog box. The Programs tab, shown in **Figure 1-20**, tab allows you to specify which program you will use for each of number of Internet services.

3 Click the arrow at the right end of the box labeled E-mail to view a list of the mail programs that are available to you. Options may include Microsoft Outlook, Hotmail, Outlook Express, Windows Messaging, or others. Select the program you want to use by clicking it.

4 Click [OK] to confirm the choice and close the Internet Options dialog box. This preference will remain in effect until you change it.

5 To activate your selected e-mail program from Internet Explorer, click the Mail button 📧 on the Standard Buttons toolbar. A menu will drop down below the button.

6 Click Read Mail (or the command that relates to the task you wish to complete) on the menu, as shown in **Figure 1-21**. Your chosen e-mail application will open. Internet Explorer will remain open, but will go to the background.

7 Close your e-mail program.

More

If your Internet connection is not active when you open the e-mail program, you may receive a prompt to establish the connection. If your e-mail program and Internet Explorer use the same Internet connection, both applications can send and receive data as part of the same session, and you can leave both open and toggle back and forth between them.

Figure 1-20 Programs tab

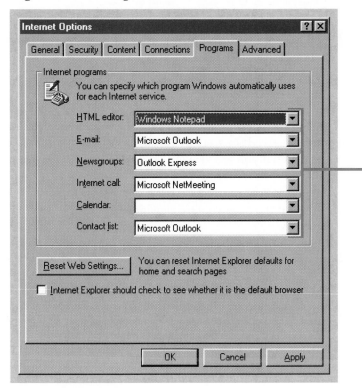

Click arrows to select a different program for a particular Internet service

Internet Explorer 5.0

Figure 1-21 Opening an e-mail program

Practice

Set Microsoft Outlook as your preferred Newsgroups program.

Hot Tip

When you click a **mailto:** hyperlink on a Web page, Internet Explorer will open an addressed message composition window in whichever program you have selected for e-mail on the Programs tab.

Checking the Properties of a Web Page

Concept

Every Web page has certain properties – its title, its URL, its file size, when it was created, and others. At times it may be useful for you to know this information, especially if you have saved the page to a disk, are working offline, and want to check where the material you are viewing originated or when it was posted.

Do It!

View the properties of the page you are viewing.

1. Click File, then click on Properties. The Properties dialog box, shown in **Figure 1-22**, appears.

2. The dialog box's General tab lists the various properties of the Web page, including protocol, document type, Internet address, file size, date created, and date modified. Review these properties to become familiar with the way in which they are expressed.

3. Click OK to close the Properties dialog box.

More

The Certificates button Certificates in the Properties dialog box relates to a security feature of Internet Explorer that you will learn more about later. Certain Web sites have files attached to them called certificates which attest to who created the site and other facts. This can be useful in evaluating the safety or validity of the content on a site. Some document types do not have certificates.

Click the Analyze button Analyze to check a page for errors that might make it load or run incorrectly. Any errors that are found will be displayed in a dialog box like the one shown in **Figure 1-23**.

Figure 1-22 Properties dialog box

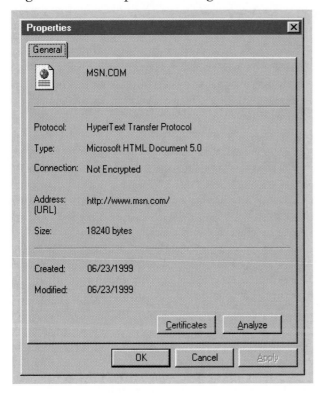

Figure 1-23 Properties dialog box

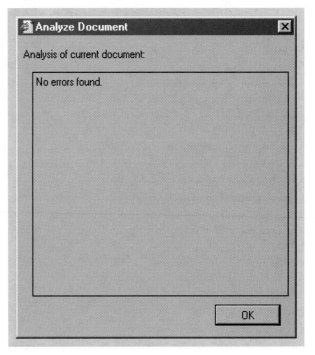

Hot Tip

Digital information is generally measured in bytes: 1,000 bytes = 1 kilobyte; 1,000 kilobytes = 1 megabyte; 1,000 megabytes = 1 gigabyte; and 1,000 gigabytes = 1 terabyte. The smallest unit of code is a bit, eight of which equal one byte.

Using the Help Feature

Concept

Internet Explorer includes a Help feature that can tell you how to perform all of the application's functions. It opens as a window that can be kept active while you follow its instructions.

Do It!

Open Internet Explorer's Help facility and use it to learn about an operation.

1 Click Help on the menu bar, then click Contents and Index. The Help window will appear.

2 You can select one of three ways to search for the information you need: the Contents tab, a list of general topics, as seen in (see **Figure 1-24**); the Index tab (see **Figure 1-25**), which provides an alphabetical list of specific functions; or the Search tab (see **Figure 1-26**), which allows you to enter a keyword that Help will try to match.

3 For this example, click the Index tab.

4 Type the phrase home page in the text box near the top of the tab. The list of topics will automatically scroll to the entry that comes closest alphabetically to what you have typed.

5 The Index contains several subtopics for home page. Click changing to select it.

6 Click the Display button Display . The frame on the right-hand side of the Help window displays the Help file for the topic you selected.

7 Read the Help file, and then close the Help window.

More

The pages of information you access through the Help facility function like little Web pages: they have hypertext links, displayed in blue underlined text, that will lead you to related topics if you click them.

The Help menu that drops down from the menu bar also contains a command called Tip of the Day. Click it to receive a randomly selected shortcut, suggestion, or cool way to use Internet Explorer!

Figure 1-24 Internet Explorer Help's Contents tab

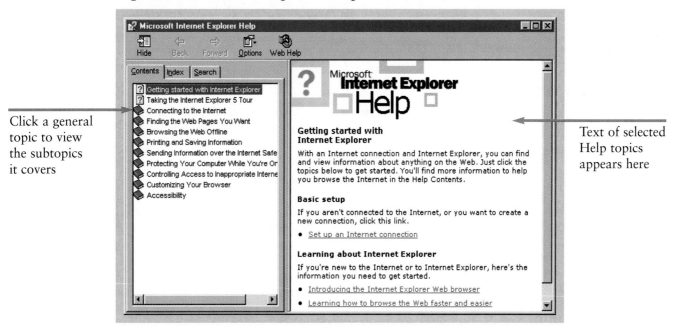

Click a general
topic to view
the subtopics
it covers

Text of selected
Help topics
appears here

Figure 1-25 Index tab

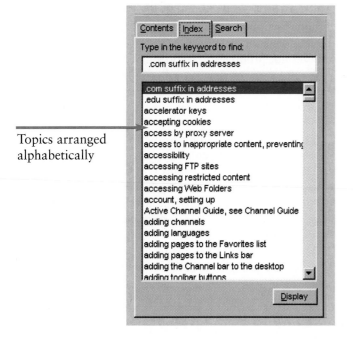

Topics arranged
alphabetically

Figure 1-26 Search tab

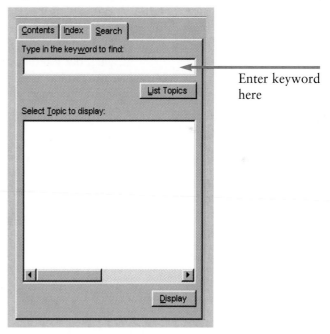

Enter keyword
here

Practice

Use Microsoft Internet Explorer Help's
Index tab to find information on the
Refresh button.

Hot Tip

If you right-click the text in the right frame
of the Help window, you can print out the
information for easy reference later. You
can also access the **Print** command by
clicking the **Options** button on the Help
toolbar.

 Exiting Internet
Explorer

Concept	When you are finished using the World Wide Web, you should close Internet Explorer and make sure your Internet connection is terminated properly.
Do It!	Close the Internet Explorer application.

   1 There are two common ways to close Internet Explorer. Either open the File menu from the menu bar and click the Close command (see **Figure 1-27**), or click the Close button ⊠ in the upper-right corner of the Internet Explorer application window.

   2 The application removes itself from the screen.

More

Users familiar with word processors, spreadsheets, and other applications may be accustomed to the need to save and close a document before exiting the application. In Microsoft Word, for example, if you attempt to close the application with an unsaved file open, you will be prompted to save the file first.

In Internet Explorer, however, there is no need to save or close the page you are viewing before exiting the application. You may wish to save the page you are viewing, but Internet Explorer will not prompt you to do so. When you exit Internet Explorer, therefore, the page you are viewing will disappear. Of course, most Web pages will still be available on the Web the next time you connect, though their content may have changed.

You will, however, have to make sure your connection to the Internet is closed properly, unless you intend to keep the session open and use an e-mail program or other application. Some Internet access providers' systems will require you to enter a logoff, while others will let you merely hang up. Closing Internet Explorer without closing the Internet connection will bring up a prompt (see **Figure 1-28**) asking if you want to sever the connection – in this case, to a service provider called BestWeb. If you are in a business or educational setting and connect to the Internet through a Local Area Network (LAN), you may be able to open and close Internet Explorer as you please without a logon or logoff procedure. Some organizations that use a LAN install their own logon systems so they can monitor Internet usage.

Figure 1-27 Closing Internet Explorer

Double-clicking the Control icon also closes the program; clicking the icon once opens a menu of commands related to the application window

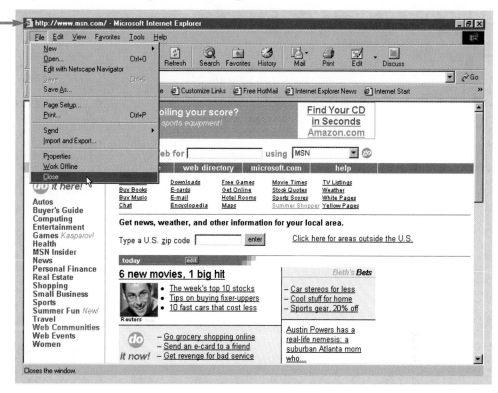

Internet Explorer 5.0

Figure 1-28 Disconnecting from the Web

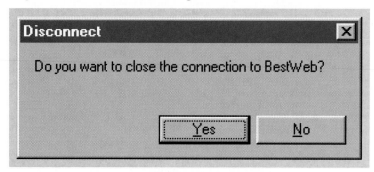

Open Internet Explorer and then close the application using a different method than the one you chose in the Do It! step.

Hot Tip

If you want to work in another application, you do not have to close Internet Explorer. Simply open the other application and Internet Explorer will go to the background. You can return to it later and your session will not have been interrupted.

Shortcuts

Function	Button/Mouse	Menu	Keyboard
Open Internet Explorer		Click Start, highlight Programs, then click Internet Explorer	
Skip forward among Address Bar, Links toolbar, and contents of current Web page	Click desired area		[Tab]
Skip backward among Address Bar, Links toolbar, and contents of current Web page	Click desired area		[Shift]+[Tab]
Return to home page		Click View, highlight Go To, then click Home Page	[Alt]+[Home]
Print current Web page		Click File, then click Print	[Ctrl]+[P]
Save current Web page		Click File, then click Save As	[Ctrl]+[S] (only to update a page you have already saved)
Open mail program		Click Tools, then highlight Mail & News, then click Read Mail	
Open Help		Click Help, then click Contents and Index	[F1]
Exit Internet Explorer		Click File, then click Close	[Alt]+[F4]

Identify Key Features

Name the items indicated by callouts in **Figure 1-29** and state their functions.

Figure 1-29 Elements of the Internet Explorer window

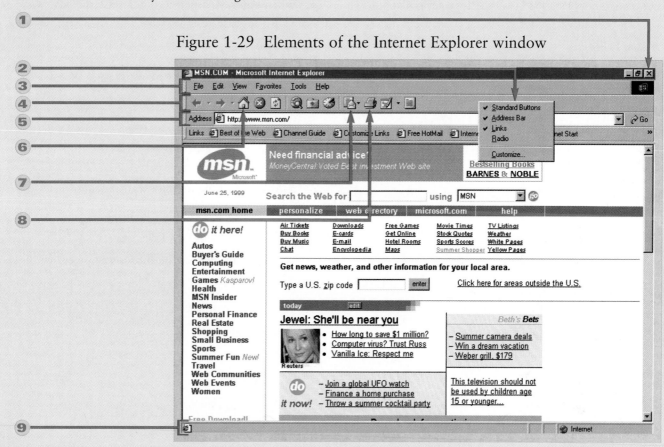

Select The Best Answer

10. Menu that gives you access to the Internet Options dialog box

11. Image, object, or text that connects you to another Web page when clicked

12. Page Internet Explorer displays automatically when it opens

13. Huge collection of linked documents you can read with Internet Explorer

14. Menu that gives you access to directions on using Internet Explorer

15. Language used to write Web pages

16. Global computer network made up of smaller networks linked together

17. Location of the Home, Print, and other useful buttons

18. Protocol used to transfer data over the Web

19. Part of the browser window that gives the URL of the current page

a. Help

b. Hyperlink

c. Standard Buttons toolbar

d. Tools

e. Address Bar

f. HTTP

g. Internet

h. Home page

i. HTML

j. World Wide Web

Quiz (continued)

Complete the Statement

20. A document's address on the Internet is also known as its:

    a. HTML

    b. URL

    c. WWW

    d. ARPA

21. The Web operates using:

    a. A local area network

    b. A government-regulated network

    c. A client-server model

    d. An array of satellites

22. When you start Internet Explorer, you will see:

    a. Your home page

    b. The Help screen

    c. Only text

    d. Only pictures

23. The Internet Explorer icon in the upper-right corner of the window spins when the program is:

    a. Done loading a Web page

    b. Seeking or loading information

    c. Saving a Web page

    d. Printing a Web page

24. To change the size of the text on a Web page, you should open the:

    a. Text Size dialog box

    b. Tools menu

    c. View menu

    d. File menu

25. When you save a page, you can use the Save Web Page dialog box to alter its:

    a. URL

    b. Name

    c. Size

    d. Certificate

26. To speed the loading of a Web page, you can:

    a. Toggle to a higher data transfer rate

    b. Turn off the display of pictures

    c. Select a smaller text size

    d. Reduce the size of the Internet Explorer window

27. To access an alphabetical list of Help topics, use the:

    a. Index tab

    b. Contents tab

    c. Search tab

    d. Advanced tab

28. You can choose your preferred e-mail program by going to the Internet Options dialog box's:

    a. Accessibility section

    b. Advanced tab

    c. General tab

    d. Programs tab

Interactivity

Test Your Skills

1. Open Internet Explorer and customize the browser window:

   a. Launch Internet Explorer from the Start menu.

   b. Move the Home button so that it is between Refresh and Stop on the Standard Buttons toolbar.

   c. Move the Address Bar below the Links toolbar.

   d. Remove the Links toolbar from view.

2. Assign a new page to serve as your browser's home page:

   a. Change your home page to http://www.altavista.com.

   b. Click the Home button to visit your new home page.

3. Change the way a page is displayed and print a paper copy of it:

   a. Change the text size on your new home page to Smallest.

   b. Change the display's background color to light green.

   c. Set your browser to repress the display of pictures.

   d. Click Refresh, and then print a copy of the entire page.

   e. Restore all of the options you just changed to their previous settings.

4. Save a Web page to your hard drive and then check the page's properties:

   a. Open the Save Web Page dialog box.

   b. Save the complete page in your My Documents folder with the name Altavista.

   c. Open the Properties dialog box for the current page.

5. Use Internet Explorer's Help facility:

   a. Open the Microsoft Internet Explorer Help window.

   b. Use the Index tab to get help on keyboard shortcuts.

   c. Attempt to locate the same help topic on the Contents tab.

   d. Close the Help window.

Interactivity (continued)

6. Terminate your work session:

   a. Reset your home page to the browser's default option.

   b. Exit Internet Explorer.

   c. If necessary, close your Internet connection.

Problem Solving

1. You work in a small real estate office. Since the World Wide Web has taken on an important role in your industry, with property listings widely available on many sites, everyone in your office has been given an Internet connection and the Internet Explorer Web browser. You are the most experienced user of the software, and your boss would like you to configure everyone's browser with a standard setup. Make the following changes to your browser: arrange the Standard Buttons toolbar so that the buttons are in alphabetical order; change the home page to http://www.lycos.com/realestate; set the browser's text size to Larger. Then, visit the new home page, print a paper copy of it, and save the page to your hard drive using the default page name.

2. You have just finished converting from another Web browser to Internet Explorer. Since you are somewhat experienced at browsing the Web, you already have some preferences as to how your browser is configured. Make these changes to your browser setup: Move the Address Bar below the Links toolbar; move the Home button to the very beginning of theStandard Buttons toolbar; set your text size to Smallest; set Hotmail as your default e-mail program. Then exit Internet Explorer.

3. You would like to prepare a document to distribute throughout your company that details some of the important features of Internet Explorer. Before writing the document, you will do some research. Use the Help facility's Contents tab to read all the help files listed under the heading Connecting to the Internet. Next, switch to the Index tab and examine help files for the following topics: adding toolbars, browser terminology, Content Advisor, security zones, and multiple browsers.

4. As a research analyst, you spend hours every day studying pages of text on the Web. Therefore, you want to maximize the amount of space available for text in your browser window. Start by removing the Standard Buttons toolbar and the Links toolbar from view. Then set the browser's text size to Smallest, and turn off the option that allows pictures to be displayed. Finally, change your home page to http://www.dol.gov, visit the page, print it, and save it your hard drive.

L E S S O N

2

BROWSING THE WEB

So far you've seen a number of ways to view and deal with pages from the World Wide Web. The real value in the Web, however, lies in the ability it gives you to move between and among different sites – "surfing" or "browsing" the Web.

Internet Explorer offers several easy and intuitive ways to navigate the practically limitless content of the Web. If you know a Web site's address, or URL, you can enter it directly. You can access a page you didn't even know existed by following a link from another page. Or, you can set a shortcut on your desktop that will allow you to go directly to a particular page with a click of your mouse.

A very convenient feature of Internet Explorer is that it remembers the last several locations you have visited during your Web session. If you follow a trail from one site to another, you can retrace your steps without having to keep notes or remember a long string of URLs.

In this section we will also examine some more ways to take information from the Web and use it for your own purposes, including saving pictures, copying text, and e-mailing URLs or even whole pages to your friends or colleagues.

Accessing a Page by Typing its URL

Concept

Each page on the World Wide Web is identified by a unique address called a URL (Uniform Resource Locator). By entering this string of characters in the Address Bar, you give Internet Explorer the data it needs to locate and retrieve the page you wish to view. Visiting a Web site in this manner requires that you know its URL ahead of time.

Do It!

Use the Address Bar to visit the Web site of the U.S. National Park Service.

1. Place the mouse pointer inside the Address Bar text box and click once to select the URL that currently resides there.

2. Type the URL http://www.nps.gov to replace the selected URL as shown in **Figure 2-1**. Be careful to copy all of the characters correctly.

3. Press [Enter] on the keyboard or click [↻Go]. Assuming your Internet connection is functioning properly, the National Park Service page will appear in your browser window (see **Figure 2-2**).

More

This is the simplest way to use a Web browser, and it will work on just about any browser application available today. Later you will learn several other methods for finding and accessing Web sites without having to type their URLs.

When people discuss Web addresses, they usually do not mention the protocol part of the URL, which is generally HyperText Transfer Protocol and is expressed as http://. It is usually okay to take the protocol for granted, though some sites do deviate from the norm and use a different protocol such as ftp (File Transfer Protocol).

Note that the last three characters of the Park Service's URL – .gov – correspond to its status as a government entity. Similarly, commercial enterprises typically have .com URLs, educational institutions have addresses ending in .edu and miscellaneous groups and nonprofit organizations tend to have URLs ending in .org. In your travels on the Web, you will also see domain names with .net suffixes for Internet related sites, and suffixes that indicate the country in which a Web server is located such as .es for Spain.

Figure 2-1 Entering a URL

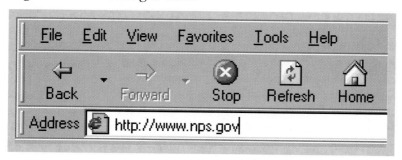

Figure 2-2 Web page for www.nps.gov

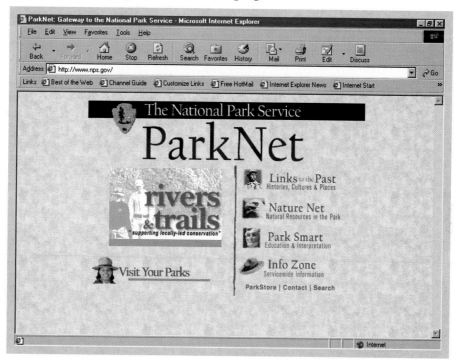

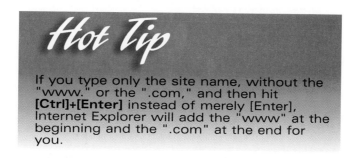

Hot Tip

If you type only the site name, without the "www." or the ".com," and then hit **[Ctrl]+[Enter]** instead of merely [Enter], Internet Explorer will add the "www" at the beginning and the ".com" at the end for you.

Accessing a Page Using Links

Concept

Most Web pages contain hyperlinks, which are pictures, objects, or segments of text that serve as "buttons" that send Internet Explorer to another Web page when you click them. Hyperlinks allow you to jump from any one place on the Web to any other without having to follow a linear path.

Do It!

On the National Park Service home page, use a hyperlink to move to another Web page featuring information about National Parks.

1. Position your mouse pointer over the text Visit Your Parks, as shown in **Figure 2-3**. Notice that the mouse pointer changes from an arrow to a hand with a pointing finger, called a Link Select pointer, and a ScreenTip appears. Also, the URL to which the link is directed, http://www.nps.gov/parks.html, is displayed in the status bar at the bottom of the browser window.

2. Click the mouse while the Link Select pointer is over the Visit Your Parks hyperlink. Internet Explorer will call up the page the hyperlink is connected to, and a page similar to the one shown in **Figure 2-4** will be loaded into the browser window. Note that the contents of the Address Bar have changed to reflect the new page.

3. Position your mouse pointer over the underlined text Preparing For Your Visit. Again, the standard mouse pointer changes to a Link Select pointer and the status bar displays the targeted URL (http://www.nps.gov/pub_aff/newvisit.html).

4. Click this link to go to the new page, which is titled The National Park Service: Preparing For Your Visit.

More

You may have noticed that the two hyperlinks you used looked different. The first was a graphic – the stylized text and the photo of the park ranger were all part of the link. The second link you used was in plain text, underlined. Links on a page can take many forms, but if the page is well designed they are seldom hard to identify.

Pages that contain many links often include the most important ones in two locations: first, scattered throughout the page wherever the page designer places them in context, and second, in a list at the bottom or along the side of the page.

Figure 2-3 Identifying a hyperlink

Link Select pointer

ScreenTip

URL of selected link

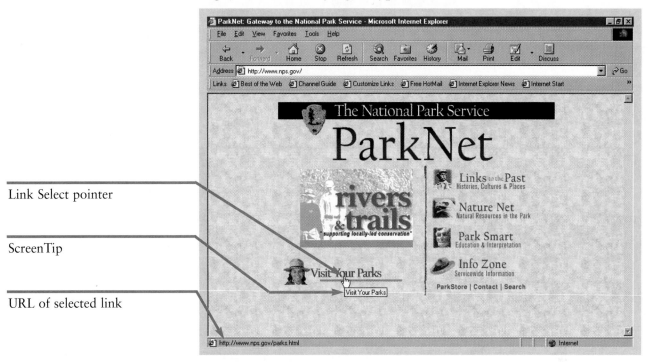

Figure 2-4 Continuing to a deeper layer of a site

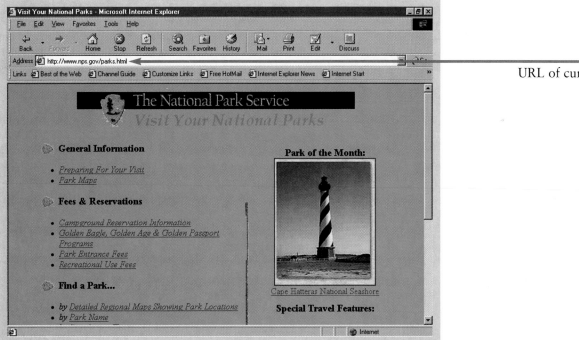

URL of current page

Hot Tip

If you wish, you can use the Colors command in the Internet Options dialog box (see Lesson 1) to specify a **hover** color. This will change the color of hyperlinks when you hold your mouse pointer over them but have yet to click.

Going Back and Forward

Concept

Often when browsing the Web you will wish to go backward – to view a page you were looking at only a moment earlier. Rather than force you to remember the URL and type it in again, Internet Explorer provides an easy way to retrace your steps. Once you have gone back, you will notice that the Forward button, which was previously "grayed out," becomes available. As you may have guessed, the Forward button enables you to revisit a page from which you have navigated back.

Do It!

With the Preparing for Your Visit page still displayed, move back to a page you viewed earlier, and then Navigate forward to the page from which you have just returned.

1. Position your mouse pointer over the Standard Buttons toolbar button labeled Back (see **Figure 2-5**).

2. Click the button to return to the Visit Your Parks page. Notice that when you go back to a page, any links on that page that you have used in the past – in this case, Preparing for Your Visit – are displayed in a different color to indicate you have already visited them.

3. Position your mouse pointer over the Forward button on the Standard Buttons toolbar (see **Figure 2-6**) and click it. The page from which you had returned, the one called Preparing for Your Visit, reappears.

More

Notice that there is a small "down" arrow to the right of the Back button. Clicking it will bring up a menu of the most recently visited pages (see **Figure 2-7**). This way, if you want to go more than one page back along the "trail" you have followed, you can do it in one step without having to click Back repeatedly. As with the Back button, the Forward button has an accompanying arrow (see **Figure 2-8**) that provides a menu of recently viewed pages (in the other direction, this time), allowing you to skip ahead several pages.

Once you have gone forward then back, you can go back and forth in both directions and see the same pages. However, if you go back, and then select a different hyperlink than the one you clicked originally, the path that had been stored in the Forward menu is replaced by the new page you entered.

Figure 2-5 Returning to a previously viewed page

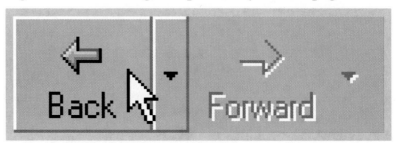

Figure 2-6 Using the Forward button

Figure 2-7 Using the Back drop-down list

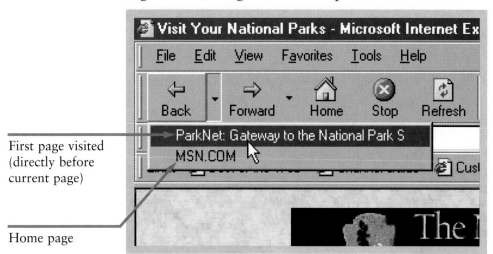

First page visited
(directly before
current page)

Home page

Figure 2-8 Forward drop-down list

Pages from which
you have
browsed back

Practice

Follow a link on the Preparing for Your Visit page, and then navigate back from the new page to the Visit Your Parks page. Finally, move forward to the Preparing for Your Visit Page again.

Hot Tip

If you right-click a nonlink area of a Web page, a small pop-up menu will appear that includes the Back and Forward commands along with many other useful commands. This can save a lot of mileage on your mouse!

 # Stopping the Loading of a Page

Concept

Sometimes when a page is in the process of loading, you will want to cancel the operation. You may have clicked the wrong hyperlink by mistake, or perhaps the loading is taking too long and you do not wish to continue. You can also utilize this when you have already received the text of a page and do not need to wait for the graphics to load.

Do It!

Stop the loading of a page before it is completed.

1 From the Visit Your National Parks page, click the hyperlink for Detailed Regional Maps Showing Park Locations under the heading Find a Park....

2 Click the Stop button ⊗ on the Standard Buttons toolbar as shown in **Figure 2-9**. If you clicked Stop early enough, the requested page will not even appear in the browser window, and the Visit Your National Parks page will remain active. If you clicked Stop after a delay, portions of the requested page may have appeared. Click the Back button to return to the Visit Your National Parks page if the latter is true.

More

When you use the Stop button to cancel a page load, any hyperlink you used to start that loading operation will change color as if you had viewed the aborted page. However, the page you almost saw will not register for either the Back or Forward commands, so if you change your mind and want to view it, you will have to click on its hyperlink again or type in its URL. If any of the requested page does appear, the page will be added to the Back and Forward menus.

Sometimes an especially long delay in loading, along with a message in the status bar that reads "Connecting to site..." and the name of the site, means Internet Explorer cannot find the site at all (see **Figure 2-10**). Eventually the application will display a message indicating that the file you are looking for cannot be displayed, but if it is taking too long, the Stop button can short-circuit the delay.

Figure 2-9 Clicking the Stop button

Figure 2-10 Failing to connect

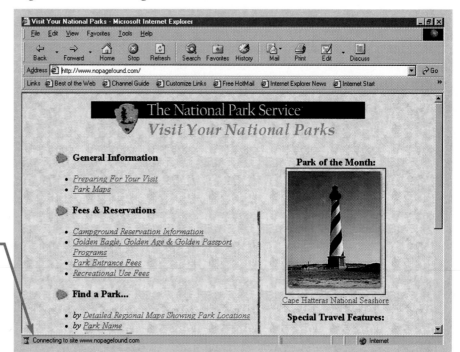

The prolonged appearance of
this message in the status bar
may indicate that the requested
page is not accessible or does
not exist

Practice

Click another hyperlink on the current page
and stop it from loading before it has a
chance to appear in the browser window.

Hot Tip

Pressing the Escape key [Esc] on the keyboard is equivalent to clicking the Stop button on the Standard Buttons toolbar.

Refreshing a Page

Concept

There may be times when you want to refresh the Web page you are currently viewing. The ability to reload a page comes in handy when it does not load correctly the first time, or when you imagine the content of the page has changed since you originally requested it.

Do It!

Refresh a page in your browser window.

1. While still on the Visit Your National Parks page, direct your browser to http://www.msn.com.

2. Position the mouse pointer over the Refresh button 🔄 on the Standard Buttons toolbar, as shown in **Figure 2-11**.

3. Click the Refresh button. The page will reload from its Web server as if you were transferring from another page. Any items that have been edited since the page was last loaded will now be updated.

4. Go back to the Visit Your National Parks page.

More

Refreshing is simple operation that might not seem very valuable at first glance, but it does have several uses. Sometimes an error in transmission will cause some of a page's content to load improperly or not at all. The Refresh button gives the page a "second chance" to load correctly. Of course, pages that suffer from faulty authoring or contain features that are not compatible with your browser will not load correctly no matter how many times you refresh them.

There are also many pages whose content changes often. For example, if your home page is a news service, you might leave the page open all day while you work with other applications, and then check in on the news page every few hours. Clicking the Refresh button will load any new news items the page's editors may have added. Some sites feature live "Webcams" that show frequently updated real-time views of scenes from around the world (see **Figure 2-12**). There are even sites that keep running scores during sporting events and update their "live coverage" several times a minute! The Refresh button helps you make the most of sites such as these.

Figure 2-11 Refreshing a page

Figure 2-12 Example of a Webcam

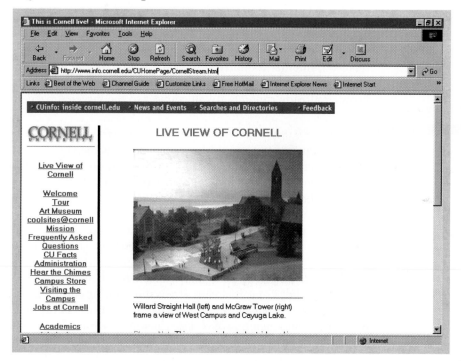

Practice

Refresh the Visit Your National Parks page.

Hot Tip

Some Webcam and live data pages are pro-grammed to refresh themselves after a set time such as 60 seconds. In some cases, you can increase the frequency of updates by refreshing the page manually.

Creating a Desktop Shortcut to a Page

Concept

The combination of Internet Explorer and the Windows operating system provides you with a way to access a Web page that is so direct, you can request the page without even having your browser running. By creating a shortcut to the page on your desktop, you can double-click the shortcut icon just as you would double-click the icon for any application or file.

Do It!

Create a desktop shortcut to the current page.

1. While viewing the Visit Your National Parks page, click File on the menu bar.

2. Position your mouse pointer over the Send command, and when a submenu appears, click Shortcut To Desktop (see Figure 2-13).

3. Now, minimize Internet Explorer and any other active applications so you can see your desktop. You should see an icon like the one in Figure 2-14. The next time you start your computer, if your Internet connection is active and you double-click this icon, Internet Explorer will launch automatically and this page will be displayed instead ot your home page. If you double-click the shortcut icon with your browser already running, it will connect to the targeted page immediately.

More

The shortcut is not a saved file of the page; it is merely a saved command that directs your computer directly to it. If you want to save the contents of a page for later viewing offline, follow the instructions for Saving a Web Page that were discussed in Lesson 1.

To remove a desktop shortcut, right-click it and select the Delete command from the pop-up menu that appears. This will send the shortcut to the Recycle Bin.

If you create a shortcut to a page whose URL then changes, the shortcut will no longer be valid. You can create a new shortcut, or edit the existing one. To edit the properties of a Web shortcut, right-click it to open its Properties dialog box. The dialog box will open to a Web Document tab, from which you can edit the URL to which the shortcut is directed, assign a shortcut key, or change the icon of the shortcut.

Figure 2-13 Creating a desktop shortcut

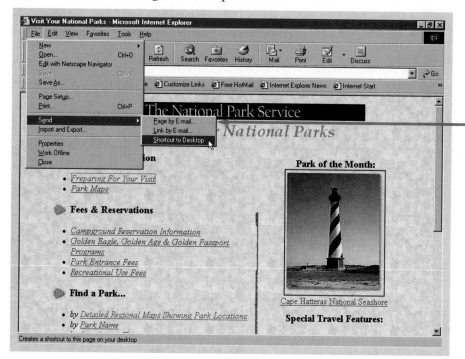

Send submenu also allows you to send current page or a link to it by e-mail

Figure 2-14 Web page shortcut on desktop

Arrow icon signifies a shortcut

Practice

Go back to another page you have visited during this lesson and create a desktop shortcut to it.

Hot Tip

Desktop shortcuts can be useful if you have a few Web pages that you need to access frequently and quickly. If you find your desktop filling up with shortcuts, consider using **Favorites**, a feature of Internet Explorer we will examine later in this text.

Copying Text from a Page

Concept

Although we have seen how to save entire Web pages, there are times when you may wish to take only a segment of text from a page and use it somewhere else. Internet Explorer allows you to do this in a manner that will be familiar to users of word processing programs such as Microsoft Word.

Do It!

Copy the address and telephone number for the Park Service from the Preparing for Your Visit page and paste it into another application. If the page has changed since this text was prepared, choose another text sample to use for this exercise.

1. Navigate your browser to the Preparing for Your Visit page on the National Park Service's Web site.

2. Position the mouse pointer at the beginning of the page's third paragraph (the one that begins with "Plan ahead."). Press down the mouse button and hold it as you drag the mouse pointer across the first line of the paragraph, highlighting it. Then drag the mouse pointer straight down to add the next two lines to the selection. The entire paragraph should be highlighted as shown in **Figure 2-15**.

3. Click Edit on the menu bar, then click Copy. The selected text has now been copied to the Windows Clipboard, a segment of your computer's memory that is used to hold small amounts of data temporarily for transfer within or between applications.

4. Click Start on the Windows taskbar, point to Programs, point to Accessories, and then click WordPad. WordPad is the Windows operating system's built-in word processor (you may also use Microsoft Word for this step).

5. Click Edit on the menu bar, then click Paste. The text you copied from the Web page is inserted into the document (see **Figure 2-16**). Save this document as Doit2-8 and then close WordPad (or Word).

More

The above example, copying an institution's contact information, is a common use of the Copy command. You may also find it handy when you are looking through large text files from which you want to retrieve only certain amounts of data, such as apartment listings, want ads, or event schedules. Data that you copy to the Clipboard will remain there until you copy something else or shut down your computer. You can paste the same piece of data from the Clipboard multiple times.

Once you have pasted the copied text into another application, you can manipulate it just as easily as if you had typed it yourself. For example, if you pasted the National Park Service's address into Microsoft Word or another word processor, you can now change its font or size, rearrange where the text lines break, add text, or delete part of what you copied.

Figure 2-15 Highlighted text on a Web page

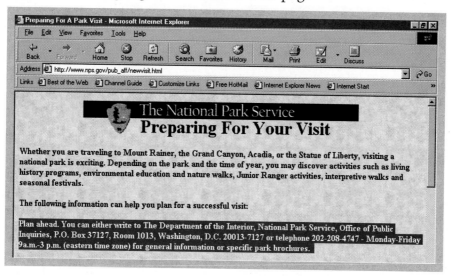

Figure 2-16 Copied text pasted into WordPad

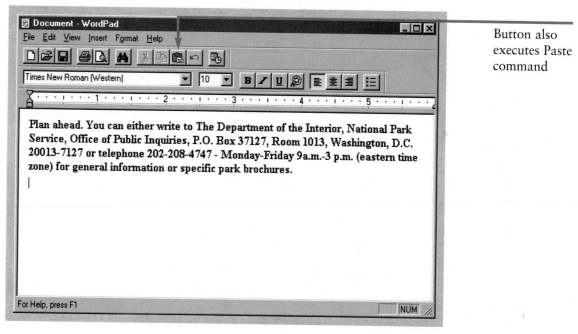

Button also
executes Paste
command

Practice

Click the Park Service's hyperlink for **park telephone numbers**. Find a park that interests you and copy its phone number.

Hot Tip

You can also copy text by right-clicking the selection. A pop-up menu will appear that includes the Copy command. This pop-up menu also permits you to print the selected text or add the remaining text on the page to the selection (**Select All**).

Saving an Image from a Page

Concept

The images displayed on Web pages are actually individual files that you can save to your computer's hard drive without saving the entire Web page. You can keep the picture files for later viewing, for use in other documents, or even to decorate your computer's desktop.

Do It!

Save the photograph of the "Park of the Month" from the Park Service's Visit Your National Parks page to your hard drive. (The photo you see will most likely differ from the one depicted in this text.)

1 Navigate back to the Visit Your National Parks page.

2 Position your mouse pointer over the photograph under the heading Park of the Month: and right-click to produce a pop-up menu (see **Figure 2-17**).

3 Click the Save Picture As command on the pop-up menu. A dialog box entitled Save Picture will appear allowing you to decide where to save the image and what to name it (see **Figure 2-18**). The My Documents folder has been selected in the Save in: box by default. If your My Documents folder includes a My Pictures folder, and you would like to save the picture in that folder, double-click it in the contents window to select it in the Save in: box. You can also use the Save in: drop-down list to select another save location if you choose.

4 The File name: box already contains the name the creator gave the image file (in this case capehatt5 for the photo of Cape Hatteras that appears in the example), but you can replace it with a name of your choosing if you wish.

5 The dialog box also gives you the option to change the file type the image will be saved as in the Save as type: box. If you are merely going to view the picture later, it is usually best to save it in the same format as it already exists. If you plan to use the file in another application, that application may require or recommend the use of a different file type. JPEG is the most commonly used format for photographs that appear on Web pages.

6 Click Save to transfer a copy of the image file to your disk.

More

The pop-up menu that contained the Save Picture As command also included a Set As Wallpaper option. Wallpaper is a Windows feature that allows you to display an image as part of your desktop: it will be there from the moment you start Windows, and will stay there until you decide to remove it. Clicking the Set As Wallpaper option on this menu will make the image that you right-clicked your desktop wallpaper. It will automatically remove any other image you had previously set as wallpaper. The options Print Target and Save Target As will be active if the image you right-clicked is also a hyperlink. The "target" is the page to which the hyperlink would send you if you clicked it, and these operations will be performed without leaving the current page. The options Open Link and Open Link in New Window will activate the hyperlink.

Figure 2-17 Picture pop-up menu

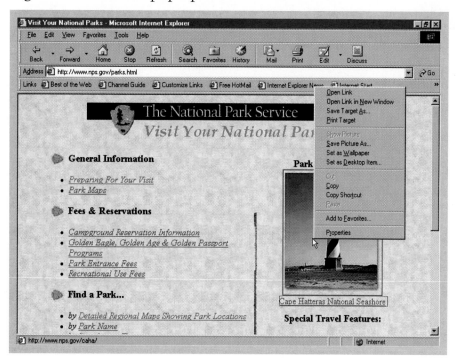

Figure 2-18 Save Picture dialog box

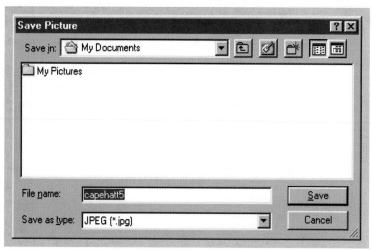

Practice

Find a picture of another national park on the National Park Service Web site and save it in the same folder as the Park of the Month photo.

Hot Tip

Despite the ease of copying text and images from the Web, remember that copyright protection may apply to the material. Do not misuse items you find on the Web.

 **AutoComplete**

Concept	Internet Explorer contains a convenient feature called AutoComplete that remembers URLs you have typed recently, senses if you are starting to type them again, and automatically finishes for you.

Do It!	Allow AutoComplete to help you type the address of the National Park Service page.

1. Click the URL currently displayed in the Address Bar to select it.

2. Begin typing http://www.nps.gov to replace the current URL as you did earlier in the lesson. If you are using the same computer you used during the earlier Skills in this book, a menu will drop down from the Address Bar about the time you type the n in nps (see **Figure 2-19**). The list will include all of the recently entered URLs that match what you have typed so far. If you continue to type, the AutoComplete options will be narrowed down as fewer match your entry exactly.

3. Click http://www.nps.gov on the AutoComplete drop-down list (see **Figure 2-20**). Your browser will take you to the page immediately. If you outsmart your computer and none of the options it presents is the one you had in mind, just keep typing in the Address Bar and enter the URL in the usual fashion.

More	AutoComplete works in other ways as well. If you have a frequently visited Web page that accepts form data – in other words, information like your name and address that you type in – AutoComplete will finish your entries in much the same way. Because some data you enter may be sensitive, such as passwords or credit card numbers, the data AutoComplete uses to finish your typing is encrypted on your hard drive. The menu options AutoComplete produces are not sent out over the Web; only the selection you choose and deliberately enter in a text box goes out to the world.

Because AutoComplete works without your having to do anything, it is not as much a "skill" as it is a feature you should prepared to encounter. In the next section we will examine ways to control the AutoComplete function, including turning it off.

Figure 2-19 AutoComplete drop-down list

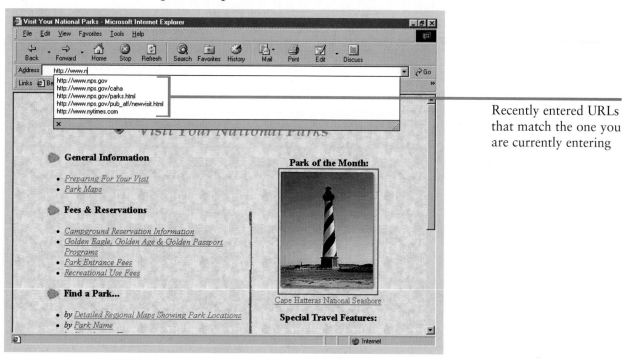

Recently entered URLs that match the one you are currently entering

Figure 2-20 Selecting a URL

Selected page will be loaded as soon as it is clicked

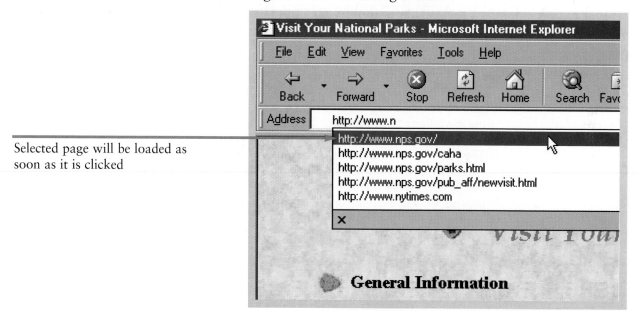

Practice

Use the AutoComplete feature to go to **http://www.msn.com**.

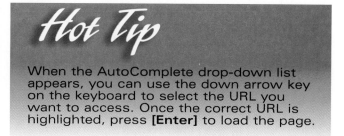

Hot Tip

When the AutoComplete drop-down list appears, you can use the down arrow key on the keyboard to select the URL you want to access. Once the correct URL is highlighted, press **[Enter]** to load the page.

Customizing AutoComplete

Concept

The AutoComplete feature you learned about in the last Skill can be tailored to meet your personal preferences. You can modify specific aspects of the feature or disable it altogether.

Do It!

Turn off the use of AutoComplete for user names and passwords on forms.

1. Open the Internet Options dialog box from the menu bar.

2. Click the Content tab to bring it to the front of the dialog box, as shown in **Figure 2-21**.

3. Click the AutoComplete button AutoComplete... in the Personal information section of the Content tab. The AutoComplete Settings dialog box, shown in **Figure 2-22**, will appear.

4. Click the check box labeled User names and passwords on forms to clear the check mark from it (if it is already unchecked, leave it that way).

5. Click OK in the AutoComplete Settings box and again in the Internet Options dialog box.

More

Until you change the settings again, AutoComplete will not function when you are filling in your name or password on a form on a Web site. You can use the same procedure to shut off AutoComplete for typing URLs in the Address Bar or for typing any information into Web forms.

The AutoComplete Settings box also gives you the option of clearing the "history" – in other words AutoComplete's stored list – of form entries and/or passwords. The history list of URLs for entry in the Address Bar is a separate record with other uses, as we will examine in the next section.

Figure 2-21 Content tab

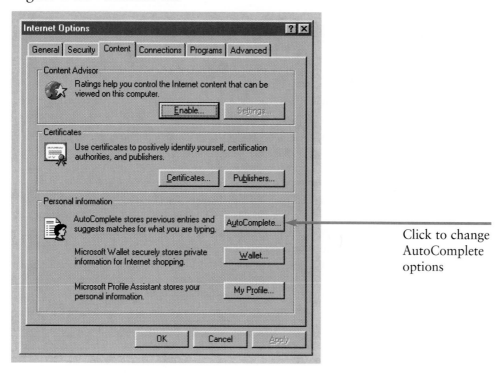

Click to change
AutoComplete
options

Figure 2-22 Selecting a URL

Clear check boxes
to deactivate
AutoComplete
options

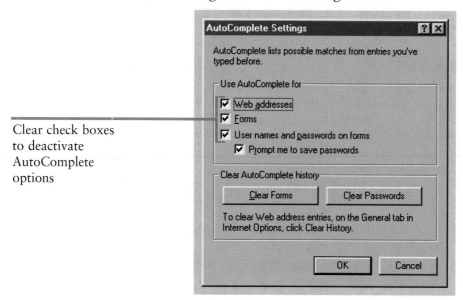

Practice

Turn AutoComplete back on for user names
and passwords on forms.

Hot Tip

You can remove an item from a list of
AutoComplete suggestions by clicking the
item and then pressing the **Delete** key.

Using the History Function

Concept

Internet Explorer will store the locations of Web sites you have visited recently, even after you have turned off your computer. This list of recently viewed sites is called your history, and you can use it to return easily to a site you have seen in the last several days.

Do It!

Access a recently visited page using the History function.

1. Click the History button on the Standard Buttons toolbar, as shown in **Figure 2-23**. The browser window will be split into two panels. The left-hand side of the browser window will be occupied by an area labeled "History" (see **Figure 2-24**). This left-hand work area is called an Explorer Bar, in this case, the History Explorer Bar, which lists active links you can click to revisit the pages you have already visited. The contents of your browser window slide to the right panel to make room for it. There are also Explorer Bars for the Search and Favorites functions, which we will explore later in this text.

2. Click any of the Web pages displayed in the History Explorer Bar to load that page into the right panel of the browser window (see **Figure 2-25**). Note that the current page (in this case Cape Hatteras NS Homepage) appears in a grayed-out form.

3. Click the History button on the Standard Buttons toolbar again to close the History Explorer Bar when you are finished using it.

More

The History Explorer Bar is organized by days. In this example, the sites visited "today" are visible. Click on another day (yours may not say "Friday" like the example) to see sites you visited on that day. Within each day are folders that contain all of the pages visited from a particular domain, or site. Click the folder icons to show and hide their contents.

If you wish to organize the contents of the History Explorer Bar in a different way, click the View button in the upper-left corner of the bar. You can choose to have your recent Web pages listed by date, by site name, by frequency of your visits, or by the order in which you visited them today.

Figure 2-23 Activating the History Bar   Figure 2-24 Using History Explorer Bar links

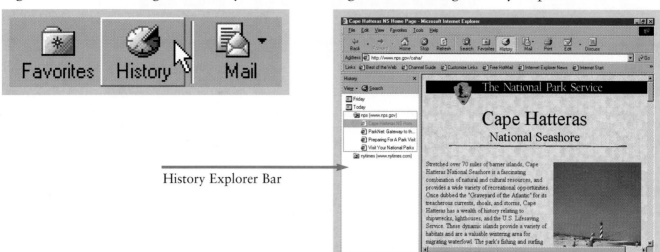

History Explorer Bar

Figure 2-25 History Bar detail

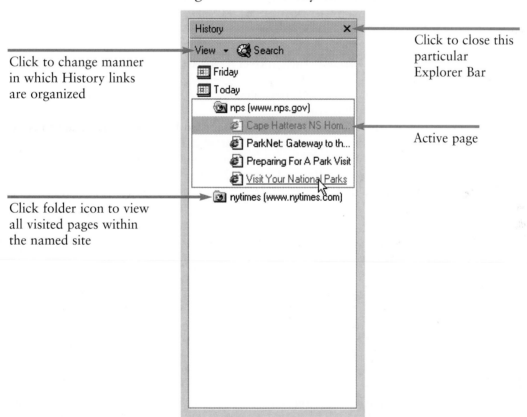

Click to change manner in which History links are organized

Click to close this particular Explorer Bar

Active page

Click folder icon to view all visited pages within the named site

Practice

Use the History Explorer Bar to visit your browser's home page. Then return to the page you just left and close the History Explorer Bar.

Hot Tip

The arrow on the right end of the Address Bar functions as an abbreviated way to access your History. Click it and a chronological list of recently visited sites will appear. You can click any of the listed sites to go to it.

Modifying Your History

Concept

When you first use Internet Explorer, the History function is set to remember the pages you have visited in the last 20 days. However, you can lengthen or reduce this amount of time. You can also remove an item from your history, or delete the entire record.

Do It!

Remove an individual page from your history, change the length of time Internet Explorer keeps pages in your history, and clear the contents of your History folder.

1. Activate the History Explorer Bar and locate the ParkNet Web page in your history. If necessary, click the appropriate day in your history and then the folder labeled nps (www.nps.gov) to reveal ParkNet in the History Bar.

2. Right-click ParkNet to produce a pop-up menu, and then click the Delete command on the menu when it appears (see **Figure 2-26**). A WARNING box will appear asking if you are sure you want to delete the history item.

3. Click [Yes]. The ParkNet listing disappears from the History Bar.

4. Open the Internet Options dialog box from the menu bar and make sure the General tab is visible.

5. In the History section of the General tab, find the spin box labeled Days to keep pages in history. If the number in the box is greater than 10, click the down arrow until it reaches 10 (see **Figure 2-27**). If the number is less than 10, click the up arrow until it reaches 10. Internet Explorer will now retain the Web pages you visit in your History folder for 10 days.

6. Click the Clear History button [Clear History], also located in the History section of the General tab. A dialog box will appear asking if you want to delete all items in your History folder.

7. Click [OK].

8. Click [OK] again in the Internet Options dialog box and close the History Explorer Bar.

More

Because items in your History folder have an "expiration date," you may not want to rely on this function for permanent storage of Web sites you want to visit again. The Favorites function you will learn about later in Lesson 4 is better suited to that purpose.

If you delete an item from your History folder, or delete the whole list, the items will be removed from the History Explorer Bar and also from the drop menu under the Address Bar.

Figure 2-26 Deleting a history item

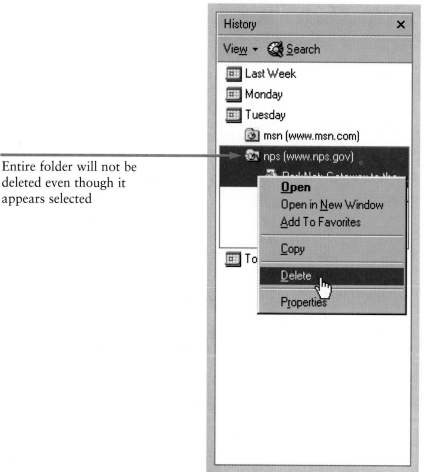

Entire folder will not be deleted even though it appears selected

Figure 2-26 Deleting a history item

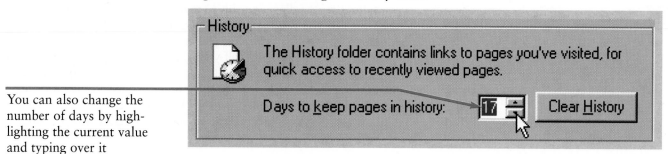

You can also change the number of days by highlighting the current value and typing over it

Practice

Adjust your History settings so Web pages are kept for 15 days.

Hot Tip

If other people have access to your computer, your History folder can allow them to see what sites you have visited. If this concerns you, you can use the History function as a safeguard for your privacy.

E-mailing a Web Page

Concept

While viewing a Web page, you may wish to share it with someone else. Internet Explorer enables you to use your default e-mail program to send the page in question as an e-mail message. This process is analogous to saving a Web page. Like many computing tasks, there is more than one way to complete this procedure, the only difference being the menus you follow to begin it.

Do It!

Prepare to send the Web page you are currently viewing via e-mail.

1. Click Tools on the menu bar, and position the mouse pointer over the Mail and News command. A submenu will appear.

2. Click the Send Page command on the submenu, as shown in **Figure 2-28**. This command will launch a new message window from the e-mail program that you have selected on the Programs tab of the Internet Options dialog box (this example uses Microsoft Outlook Express).

3. When the message window opens, the page you were viewing will appear in the body section (see **Figure 2-29**). The Subject line in the addressing area will contain the name of the page. All you have to do is enter the e-mail address of the intended recipient and click the Send button.

4. You can perform this same operation by clicking the Mail button on the Standard Buttons toolbar and then clicking Send Page on the menu appears, or by opening the File menu, higlighting the Send command, and clicking Page by E-mail on the submenu that appears.

More

The different procedures for sending a page by e-mail also include an option for sending a link by e-mail. If you send someone a link, he or she will receive an e-mail message containing the URL of the page you are currently visiting. The URL you send will arrive as an active hyperlink: if your recipient has an Internet browser and a valid Internet connection, he or she will be able to access the page simply by clicking the URL in the body of the e-mail message. Before you send the message, you can type additional information along with the URL, just as you would type an ordinary e-mail message (such as "Hey, Jane, I thought you might enjoy this site! Love, Bob").

If you are trying to decide whether to send someone a whole page or just the link, consider whether that person has his or her own access to the Web. If not, you should send the whole page. Also, if the page changes frequently and you want your recipient to see something that is on it right now, send the page. If you send the link, your recipient will see the page as it exists later, not necessarily what you saw.

Figure 2-28 Send Page command

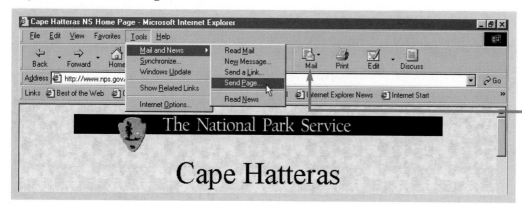

Send Page command also available by clicking Mail button

Figure 2-29 E-mailing a Web page with Outlook Express

Click to e-mail page

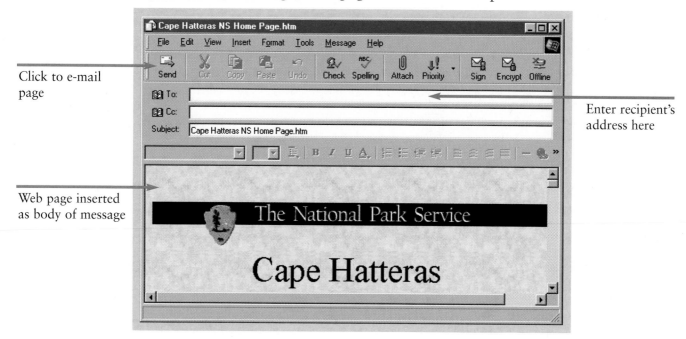

Enter recipient's address here

Web page inserted as body of message

Practice

E-mail the page you are currently viewing to a friend. If you do not have the address of a friend with you, send the page to yourself as a test.

Hot Tip

In order for Web pages to be sent and received in this manner, both parties must be using mail programs that are capable of displaying HTML documents. Otherwise, you will have to save the Web page and e-mail it as an attached file.

Shortcuts

Function	Button/Mouse	Menu	Keyboard
Add **www.** before, and **.com** after, a site name in the Address Bar			[Ctrl]+[Enter]
Select the current URL in the Address Bar	Click inside Address Bar text box		[Alt]+[D]
Browse back to previous page	⬅	Click View, highlight Go To, then click Back	[Alt]+[Left Arrow]
Browse forward to last page viewed	➡	Click View, highlight Go To, then click Forward	[Alt]+[Right Arrow]
Open Address Bar drop-down history menu	▼		[F4]
Stop the loading of a page	⊗	Click View, then click Stop	[Esc]
Refresh the current page	⟳	Click View, then click Refresh	[F5]
Copy highlighted text to Clipboard		Click Edit, then click Copy	[Ctrl]+[C]
Paste text from Clipboard		Click Edit, then click Paste	[Ctrl]+[V]
Highlight all text on a page		Click Edit, then click Select All	[Ctrl]+[A]
Activate History Explorer Bar	🧭	Click View, highlight Explorer Bar, then click History	[Ctrl]+[H]

Identify Key Features

Name the items identified by callouts in **Figure 2-30**.

Figure 2-30 Elements associated with Web browsing

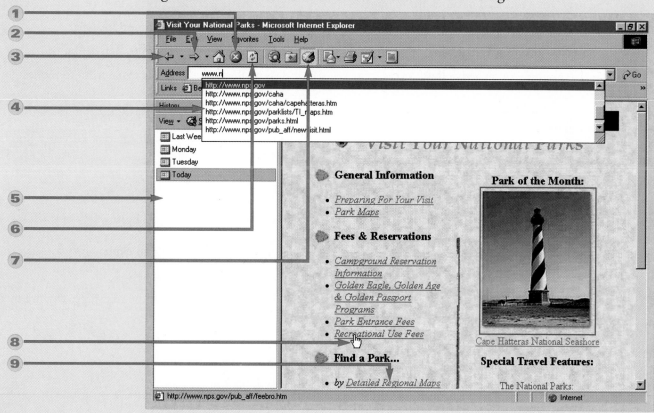

Select The Best Answer

10. Remembers URLs you have typed recently and helps you enter them

11. Creates an e-mail message that includes the contents of the current page

12. Brings up the most recently viewed page

13. An image you install as part of your dekstop

14. Reloads the contents of the current page

15. An icon you create on your desktop to call up a Web page

16. Brings up the page from which you have just retraced your steps

17. Creates an e-mail message that includes the URL of the current page

18. Remembers pages you have visited recently and helps you recall them

19. Interrupts the loading of a page

a. Forward button

b. Shortcut

c. Refresh button

d. Wallpaper

e. Send Page command

f. Back button

g. AutoComplete

h. History

i. Send Link command

j. Stop button

Quiz (continued)

Complete the Statement

20. The mouse pointer changes to a hand with a pointing finger to indicate that:

    a. The page you requested has finished loading

    b. The link you are pointing to is a Favorite

    c. You must wait for a page to load

    d. You are pointing to an active link

21. The Stop button:

    a. Terminates your Internet connection

    b. Terminates the loading of a page in progress

    c. Pauses the loading of a page in progress

    d. Deactivates animations on the current page

22. By creating a desktop shortcut, you:

    a. Set up a way to start Internet Explorer by calling up a particular page

    b. Make it possible to view your desktop without exiting Internet Explorer

    c. Copy items to your desktop from the History folder

    d. Extend the AutoComplete feature to the desktop

23. When you save an image from a page, you can:

    a. Put it in a folder on your hard drive

    b. Print it

    c. Set it as your desktop wallpaper

    d. All of the above

24. If you think the contents of a Web page may have changed since you last accessed it, you should:

    a. Check to see whether it is in your History folder

    b. Type today's date in the Address Bar

    c. Reload the page using the Refresh button

    d. E-mail the site the page came from to request an update

25. When viewing a page with Internet Explorer, you cannot directly e-mail:

    a. The page's URL

    b. The page's text

    c. The full content of the page

    d. The page's URL with an explanatory message

26. When visiting a page for the first time, you are most likely to use:

    a. AutoComplete

    b. Your history

    c. A hyperlink

    d. The Forward button

27. AutoComplete:

    a. Inserts characters in the Address Bar that you have not typed yet

    b. Makes a list of your recently viewed pages available to others on the Internet

    c. Makes your personal information available to others on the Internet

    d. Connects you to the Internet before you finish the dial up procedure

Interactivity

Test Your Skills

1. Visit and explore a Web site:

   a. Use the Address Bar to visit the home page of the National Weather Service at http://www.nws.noaa.gov.

   b. Use the hyperlink on the National Weather Service home page to visit the Warnings page.

   c. From the Warnings page, click the Show All hyperlink.

   d. Stop the All Warnings page before it finishes loading.

   e. Navigate back to the National Weather Serivce home page.

   f. Go forward again to the Warnings page and refresh it.

   g. Return to the home page.

2. Work with a Web page:

   a. Create a desktop shortcut to the National Weather Service home page.

   b. Scroll down to the bottom of the home page and highlight the mailing address text for the National Weather Service at the bottom of the page.

   c. Copy the highlighted text to the Clipboard.

   d. Open WordPad from the Start menu and paste the text you copied.

   e. Save the NOAA (National Oceanic and Atmospheric Administration) logo image to your hard drive.

   f. E-mail the National Weather Service home page to a friend or yourself.

3. Use AutoComplete and the History Explorer Bar:

   a. Allow AutoComplete to help you access the National Weather Service's Warnings page.

   b. Activate the History Explorer Bar.

   c. Use the History Bar to go to the All Warnings page.

   d. Set your History folder to retain pages for 14 days.

   e. Close the History Explorer Bar.

Interactivity (continued)

Problem Solving

1. Browsing Challenge: Use the Address Bar to go to www.altavista.com. Then, using hyperlinks only, navigate to the following Web sites:

   a. CNN/SI or ESPN (Sports & Recreation)

   b. Shareware.com (Computers & Internet)

   c. Ask NOAH (Health & Fitness)

   d. Shopping.com

2. You are scheduled to lead a tour of a construction site for your company's new building three days from now. Since much of the tour will be spent out in the open, you want to make sure that the weather forecast is good. Starting from www.msn.com, access a weather report for the closest major city to your current location. When you reach a page with the extended forecast, refresh it to make sure you have the most up to date information. Then create a desktop shortcut to the page. Finally, copy the text of the forecast and paste it into a WordPad document. Save the WordPad document using the file name PS2-2.

3. The Director of Marketing in your company has asked you to survey several Web sites to see what types of advertisements they include. Use a combination of links and URLs you know to visit some of the commercial sites you have seen so far. Scan these pages for advertisements that include images. Save at least three of the images you see to your hard drive. Also create desktop shortcuts to the pages on which the images reside. If you have an active e-mail account, send one of the pages you have discovered to a friend as an e-mail message.

4. You have just completed a research project and are now ready to move on to your next assignment. You have visited a great number of Web pages over the last while, and your History folder has become quite cluttered. It would probably be a good idea to clear the folder before beginning the new project, but first you should check to see if any of the pages you have visited will still be useful. Activate the History Explorer Bar and review all the sites and pages you have visited since your history was last cleared by clicking the day and week icons. Revisit at least one page from each time slot. Delete the page you visited most recently from your history. Then, clear your entire history and reset the number of days pages will remain in it to 25.

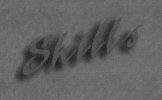

L E S S O N

3

SEARCHING THE WEB

O f all the feats you can perform on the World Wide Web, perhaps the most impressive is searching – finding Web pages you did not know about before, in order to look up facts, answer questions, or just have fun.

So far, we have learned how to access Web sites that we already knew how to find, either because we knew their URLs or because they were made available through hyperlinks. So, how do you find a Web site without those clues? The key lies in using special Web sites, called search engines, designed expressly for searching. You may have heard of commercial sites such as Yahoo, Infoseek, Hot Bot or Lycos. Microsoft has its own page for searching. You can use any search site, and more are appearing all the time.

To use one of these search engines, the user typically enters a key-word or question. The site will return a list of Web pages (presented as hyperlinks) that appear to satisfy the request, and the user can click one to go to that page. Voilà, you're somewhere on the Web you didn't even know existed before. Search engines appear to work by magic, but the people who run them spend all their time canvas-sing the huge content of the Web, looking for new sites and entering them into large databases according to the topics they cover.

With early Web browsers, people accessed search engines the same way they accessed any other page: by entering the URL and getting busy. More recent browsers have featured a "search" button that would take you directly to a particular search site. Internet Explorer has a comprehensive search function called the Search Assistant that allows you to use multiple search engines, organize which engines you use for different kinds of searches, and save the results of the searches you have performed. The Search Assistant's usefulness goes beyond finding Web sites; through the use of specialized search engines, it can help you find people, businesses, maps, newsgroup postings, or even entries in Microsoft's own encyclopedia.

Internet Explorer also features a shortcut way to search using the Address Bar. And if you feel like it, you can always type in the address of your favorite search engine manually, just like in the wild old days of the mid-1990s.

The Search Assistant

Concept

The Search Assistant is a feature of Internet Explorer that helps you conduct, customize, organize, and save searches on the Web. It functions through an Explorer Bar, similar to the one you used for the History function.

Do It!

Activate Internet Explorer's Search Explorer Bar.

1 Click the Search button on the Standard buttons toolbar as shown in **Figure 3-1**.

2 The Search Explorer Bar opens on the left-hand side of the browser window, and the other contents of the browser window slide to the right to make room for it, as shown in **Figure 3-2**.

More

As you can see in **Figure 3-3**, the Search Explorer Bar includes several categories of searches, each of which is accompanied by a radio button. Click on each of them and notice how the lower half of the Search Bar changes, prompting you for different search information for each category.

Below the listed categories is a hyperlink for More..., which, if clicked, will make additional search categories available. Find in Encyclopedia will start a search on Microsoft's Encarta encyclopedia, and Find in Newsgroups will start a search among the many specialized Usenet newsgroups, which are electronic bulletin boards that allow Internet users to exchange ideas and have discussions about particular topics of interest to them.

Figure 3-1 Activating the Search Bar

Figure 3-2 Active Search Bar

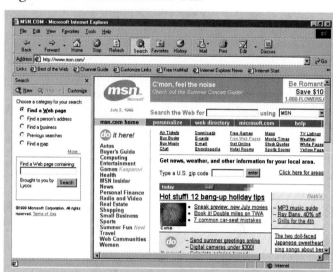

Figure 3-3 Search Bar detail

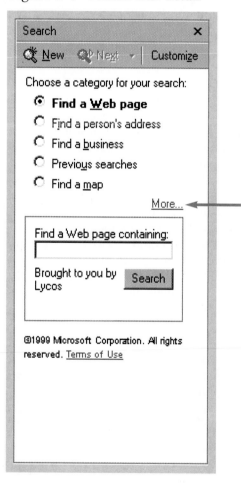

Click hyperlink
to access more
search categories

Hot Tip

Accessing the engines and services of the
Search Assistant is like accessing anything
else on the Web. Your Internet connection
must be active and valid before you proceed.

Finding Web Pages Using the Search Explorer Bar

Concept

Finding a Web site on a selected topic using the Search Assistant is a simple matter of entering the necessary information in the Search Explorer Bar and letting Internet Explorer do the work. The Search Assistant will look up your keyword on a variety of available online resources; in a later section you will learn how to control which services it uses for each category of search.

Do It!

Find a Web site that contains information about early American explorers Lewis and Clark.

1. With the Search Explorer Bar open, look at the radio button next to the category named Find a Web Page. If it is not filled, in, click it so that a dot appears.

2. In the text box labeled Find a Web page containing:, type Lewis and Clark, as in **Figure 3-4**.

3. Click the Search button ⬛ Search . After a few moments elapse, a list of search results from a particular search engine will appear in the Search Bar similar to the one pictured in **Figure 3-5**. Note that the list you see may be different, as the Web is changing constantly.

4. The results are displayed as hyperlinks. Click a link that looks promising to open that page in the browser window as in **Figure 3-6**. The Search Explorer Bar and its contents will remain intact, allowing you to check out several of the search results without having to conduct the search again or return to a search page each time. In fact, if you close the Search Bar, the results will still be there if you activate it again during your work session. As with links in other situations, the search results you have already visited will appear in a different color in the Explorer Bar.

More

You have just opened Pandora's Box. There are a few important features you should note about the results display, but the first thing you are likely to see is the number of pages your search found. In our example it is almost two million. You will also see that the pages presented to you have varying degrees of relevance to your topic. In fact, though it is not shown in this example, some search engines display their results in order of "relevance," which is a statistical expression of how closely each result matches your search criteria. If you are trying to learn about the people who traveled across the newly acquired Louisiana Territory in 1804–1806, for example, you probably are not interested in the Lewis-Clark State College, but there it is. Learning to craft your inquiries to get relevant returns (and learning how to deal with the irrelevant returns you will get anyway) is a skill you will develop over time.

Some search engines allow you to control how many results are displayed at a time. Most include a list of hyperlinked page numbers that enable you to view more results if the first set is not satisfactory. Others search engines let you expand each result so that it includes a description instead of just a one line hyperlink. Since space in the Search Bar is limited, you can point to a hyperlink to receive a ScreenTip containing a description of the page to which the result is linked.

Figure 3-4 Entering a search string

Figure 3-5 Results of a search

Click Next to run same search with a different search engine

Click Next arrow to run search with a specifc engine

Click to view next page of results

Figure 3-6 Viewing a search result

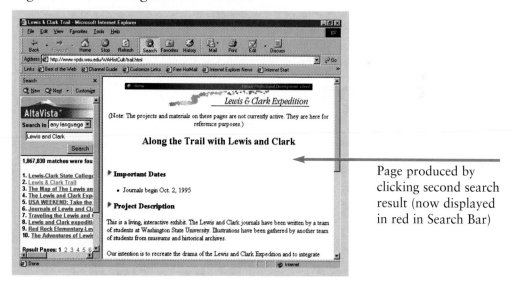

Page produced by clicking second search result (now displayed in red in Search Bar)

Practice

Follow several of the links produced by the Lewis and Clark search. Then conduct a search for Web pages that discuss the **Lousiana Purchase**.

Hot Tip

You can use logical operators such as "and" and "or" in your search string to refine your Web searches. Also use "+" to require a word in or "-" to a exclude a word from the search results.

 # Searching for Other Types of Information

Concept

Though in reality all Web searches technically involve finding Web pages, the contents of some Web sites are specialized enough that Internet Explorer categorizes them differently in the Search Explorer Bar. Searches for individuals, companies, and maps are handled with special screens of their own.

Do It!

Search for a map using the Search Explorer Bar.

1 With the Search Explorer Bar still displaying your last search results, click the button labeled with the word New and an icon of a magnifying glass (see **Figure 3-7**). The original Search Assistant choices will reappear.

2 Click the radio button labeled Find a map. A new set of text boxes will appear.

3 Leave the Search For: selection box set to Address (you can also choose places or landmarks). Then click inside the This Address: text box and type 1600 Pennsylvania Avenue.

4 Press [Tab] to activate the City: text box and type Washington. Then press [Tab] again and type DC in the State/province text box. Notice that, as in **Figure 3-8**, you do not have to enter data for every field in the form, but the more specific you are, the more accurate your results are likely to be.

5 Click Search to access a map for the requested address from Microsoft's proprietary database called Expedia Maps. The resulting map that appears in the right half of the browser window should be similar to the example shown in **Figure 3-9**.

More

As with any Web site, the map page you have accessed contains a host of options you can activate with links. Once you are at a Web site that is the result of a search, you can follow links to your heart's content and leave the Search Assistant far behind. If the Search Assistant cannot match your map request exactly, you will be presented with a list of hyperlinked alternatives in the Explorer Bar.

You can see that part of the map you have found is obscured. Remember that by clicking the Standard Buttons toolbar's depressed Search button you can close the Search Explorer Bar, and the Web page will slide back and take over the whole browser window. If you click to open the Search Bar again before exiting Internet Explorer, your search results will still be there.

Figure 3-7 Starting a new search

Figure 3-8 Searching for a map

Figure 3-9 Expedia map

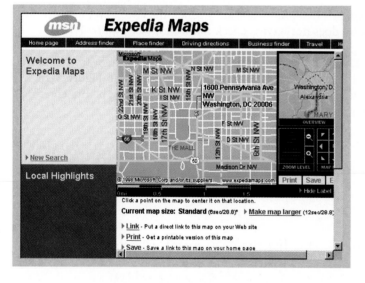

Practice

Search for a map using your home address.

Hot Tip

The Search Assistant options for finding people and businesses work very similarly. To try these out, click the **New** button in the Explorer Bar, select the appropriate radio button and enter the required information.

 **Customizing the Search Assistant**

Concept

The search categories available in the Search Assistant are not set in stone. You can decide which categories appear in the Search Explorer Bar when you call it up, and in which order. This option is particularly helpful for users whose search habits and needs are consistent.

Do It!

Change the search categories displayed by the Search Assistant, remove a search engine from a category, and then change the order in which engines are consulted.

1 Click the Customize button near the top of the Search Explorer Bar (see **Figure 3-10**). A new window titled Customize Search Settings will appear (see **Figure 3-11**). This is the control center for your Search Assistant. The window is divided into categories for each of the different kinds of searches you can perform. Next to each main category is a check box that allows you to determine whether that category is included in the Search Assistant. Below the category heading is a list box that displays all of the search engines available for the category, in the order they will be used. Next to the list box is a series of check boxes. Search engines that are checked are currently active in your Search Assistant. Only a few categories are visible at once, but you can scroll down to view more.

2 Scroll down to the category titled Find a Business. Click the check box next to the category name so the box does not have a check mark in it (see **Figure 3-12**).

3 Click the OK button [OK] at the bottom of the window. The Search Explorer Bar will be reloaded without the Find a business radio button, as in **Figure 3-13**. The browser window will return to the page you had been viewing before entering the customizing function.

Figure 3-10 Starting the customization process

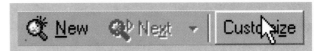

Figure 3-11 Customize Search Settings window

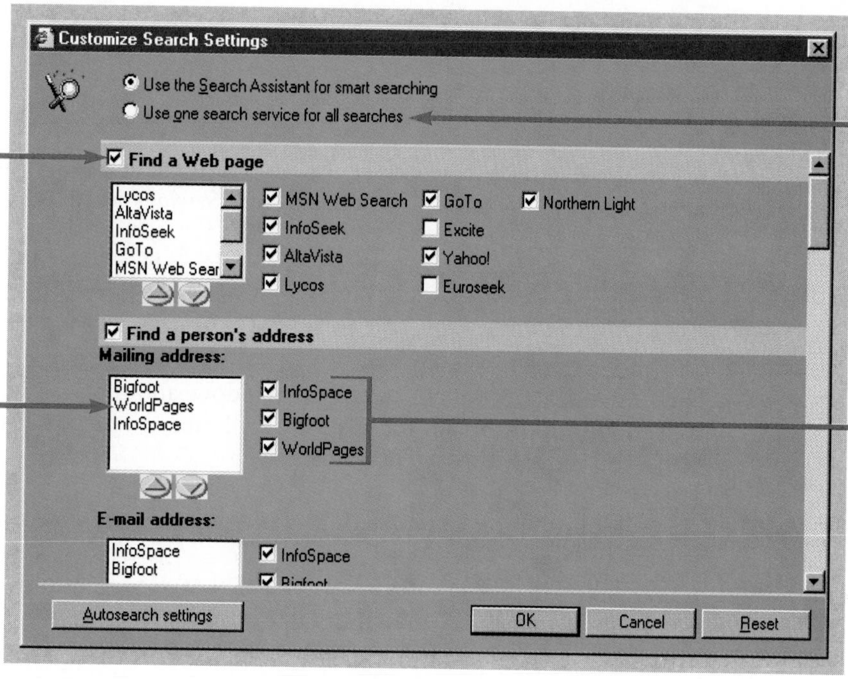

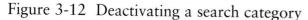

Remove check mark to remove category from Search Assistant

List of all services available for this category of search

Selecting this option leaves one list from which you can choose one service for all searches

Check marks indicate that all available services for this category are active in the Search Assistant

Figure 3-12 Deactivating a search category

Figure 3-13 Customized Search Bar

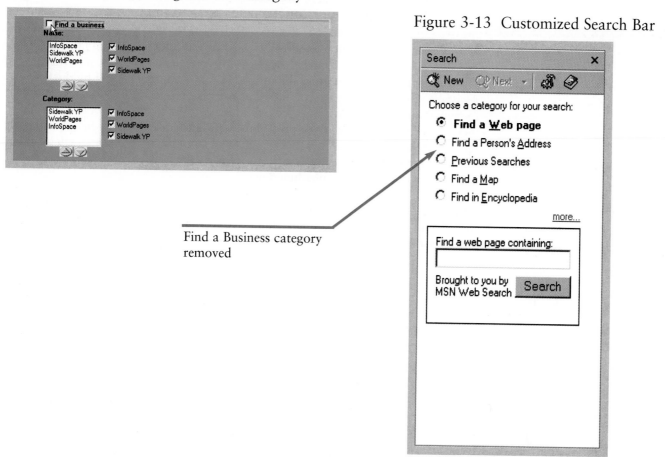

Find a Business category removed

Customizing the
Search Assistant
(continued)

Do It!

4 To remove a particular search engine from a search category, click the Customize button again to open the Customize Search Settings window.

5 In the Find a Web page category, click the check box labeled Lycos to remove the check from it (see Figure 3-14). Lycos disappears from the list of search engines to the left.

6 Click [OK] at the bottom of the window, and the Search Assistant will reset itself. Any future searches for Web sites will not include the Lycos search engine unless you restore it to active status.

7 Open the Customize Search Settings window one more time.

8 In the Find a Web page category, click MSN Web Search to select it in the list of active search engines, as shown in Figure 3-15.

9 Click the Move Up button ⬆ below the list twice. MSN Web Search moves up two places in the list (see Figure 3-16).

10 Click [OK] to close the Customize Search Settings window and confirm the new search engine order. In any future searches for Web sites, MSN Web Search will be the second search engine accessed by the Search Assistant.

More

Note that the customization window gives you a radio button option labeled Use one search service for all searches. If you would prefer simply to use a particular search engine all the time rather than the multifold resources offered by the Search Assistant, click that option and follow the instruction to choose a search engine. Examples are InfoSeek, Yahoo, Lycos, HotBot, AltaVista, and many others. All of these are privately managed, for-profit businesses. You use them for free, but they sell advertising that you see on their pages. Several of the named search engines are used in more than one category by the Search Assistant because these services are able to perform more than one function.

As with screen colors and fonts, the options of the Search Assistant are best left on their default settings until you have familiarized yourself with the search process and have established usage patterns of your own.

Figure 3-14 Deactivating a search engine

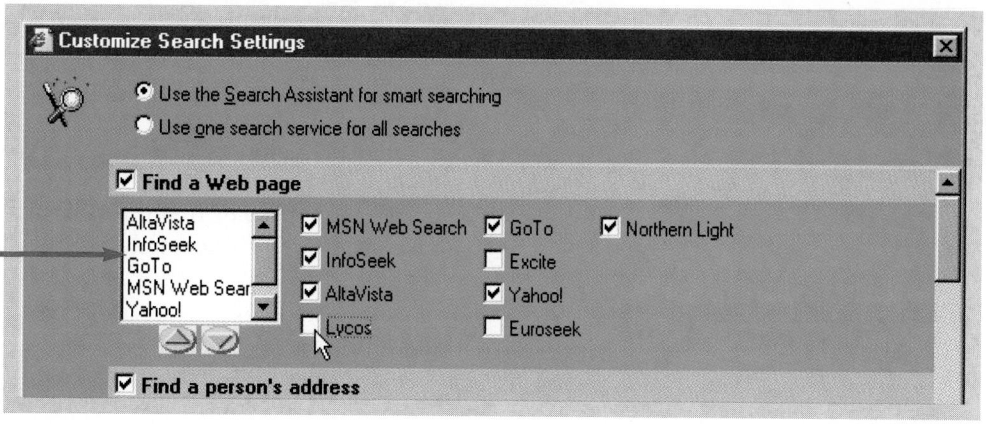

Lycos no longer appears
in list of search engines
available for finding
Web sites

Figure 3-15 Selecting a search engine to move

Figure 3-16 New search engine order

Practice

Restore the **Find a business** category to
active status. Also restore the **Lycos**
search engine in the Find a Web site category, and move it to fourth in the order in
the list of active search engines for that
category.

Hot Tip

If you have made several changes to the
Search Assistant settings and want to
return to Internet Explorer's default settings, you can click the **Reset** button at
the bottom of the customization window.

Using Previous Search Results

Concept

If you so choose, Internet Explorer's Search Assistant will save the results of previous searches and allow you to recall them. This can be useful if you have to interrupt your Web browsing session, or if you revisit an earlier research topic and want to be sure you are consulting the same material.

Do It!

Set the Search Assistant to save the results of your previous 10 searches, and recall the results of a previous search.

1 With the Search Explorer Bar open, click the Customize button. The Customize Search Settings window will appear.

2 Scroll down to the category named Previous searches (see **Figure 3-17**).

3 Look to see if there is a check mark in the check box next to Previous searches. If not, click the check box to place a check mark in it.

4 Click [OK] at the bottom of the window.

5 In the Search Explorer Bar, click the radio button labeled Previous searches. A menu of your recent searches will appear as a list of hyperlinks (see **Figure 3-18**).

6 Click the hyperlink for the Lewis and Clark search you performed a short time ago, and the results of that earlier search will appear. You can utilize those search results in the same way you did when you first conducted the search.

7 Close the Search Explorer Bar.

More

Search results are saved as files – they are not searched for all over again when you recall them, so any changes you have made to customize the Search Assistant since making the search will not be reflected in the saved search results. For example, if you conduct a search and receive results from the Infoseek search engine, then customize the Search Assistant so that Infoseek is no longer consulted, the Infoseek results will still be there when you recall the saved search results. This also means that if new information on your topic has become available on the Web since you originally made your search, it will not show up in the recalled search.

Figure 3-17 Previous searches category

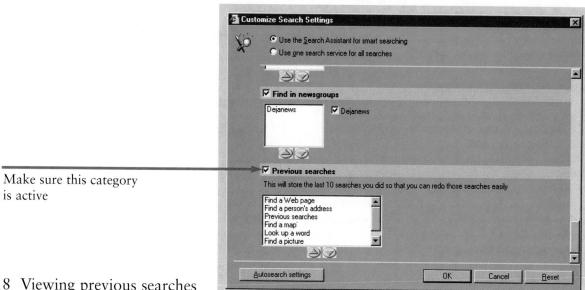

Make sure this category
is active

Figure 3-18 Viewing previous searches

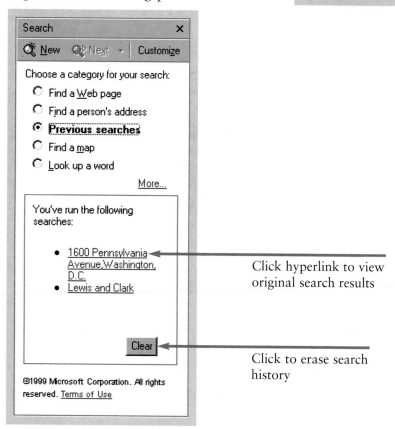

Click hyperlink to view
original search results

Click to erase search
history

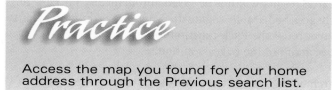

Practice

Access the map you found for your home
address through the Previous search list.

Hot Tip

The Search Assistant cannot save more
than the last 10 searches. If you find a
page you like in a search and want to save
its location more permanently, the best
way to do so is by using the **Favorites**
function we will discuss in the next lesson.

Accessing a Search Engine Directly

Concept

As you have seen in using the Search Assistant, there are many search engines and information services available on the Web. These are not part of Internet Explorer, and most of them are private companies that have no connection with Microsoft. Each of them has its strengths and weaknesses, and each of them functions a little differently. The Search Assistant automatically uses many of them at once for each of your searches, but you may wish to bypass the Search Assistant and go directly to one of these sites – either because it provides specialized help in an area of interest to you, or simply because you find it more comfortable to use.

Do It!

Access the Lycos search engine directly, without using the Search Assistant.

1 Click the current URL in the Address Bar to select it and type in the URL for Lycos, www.lycos.com over it. Then click ⟨Go⟩ or press [Enter].

2 If your Internet connection is active, the Lycos page will load into your browser window like any other Web page, as in **Figure 3-19**.

3 Lycos is typical of many commercial search engines in that it offers a variety of "extras" such as news headlines, Internet tools, and direct links to specific kinds of information. But like all search engines, it is built around a general search function with a text box and an execute button (in this case, Go Get It!).

4 Type "Web browsers" in the search text box (see **Figure 3-20**) and click the Go Get It! button **Go Get It!** . In most search engines, the [Enter] key will work as well.

5 A page of search results (like those in **Figure 3-21**) will appear that resembles the ones you have seen in the Search Explorer Bar, except it will fill the whole browser window (you may have to scroll down the page to see the results). You can click the links provided and access the found pages in the same way you did earlier.

More

When you use a search engine in this way, you will almost always find yourself in a commercial environment. Note the many ads, offers of services, and other "extras" pasted into the results page you just called up. Caveat emptor. On the other hand, many of the sites offer powerful search functions. The Lycos page is like many others in that the results page features a Search These Results option: you can enter more keywords and narrow the search you already made rather than starting a new search from scratch.

Several of the advantages of the Search Assistant are not available when you search using this method. Your search results will not be saved automatically for later reference. Also, since a directly accessed search engine does not use an Explorer Bar to split the screen, you will have to use the Back function to return to the results list after having looked at one or more of the pages you find.

If you find a particular search engine you like so much you want to use it all the time, you can customize the Search Assistant so that clicking Search on the Standard Buttons toolbar will open an Explorer Bar directly to that site instead of activating the traditional Search Assistant options.

Figure 3-19 Lycos home page

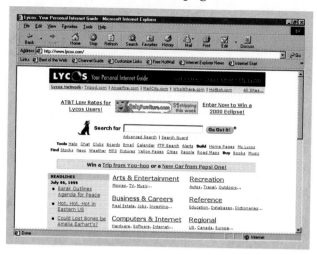

Figure 3-20 Searching on Lycos' home page

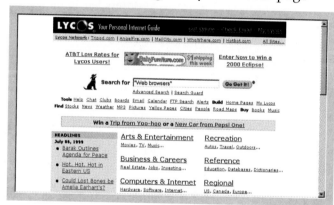

Figure 3-21 Lycos search results

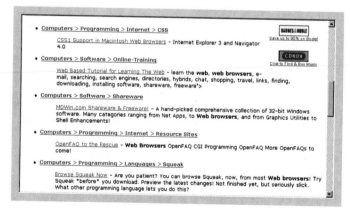

Visit the search sites at **www.excite.com**, **www.yahoo.com**, and **www.hotbot.com**, and search for "Web browsers" at each site. Compare and contrast the different search sites and the results they return.

Enclosing a search phrase in quotations instructs the search engine to return only those Web pages that contain the exact phrase.

Searching Using the Address Bar

Concept

Here is a trick that even some veteran Web surfers do not know about. For a quick, simple keyword search of the Web, you can enter your search criteria in the Address Bar preceded by "go," "find" or "?" and Internet Explorer will begin a search using its preset search service, MSN Autosearch.

Do It!

Search the Web from the Internet Explorer Address Bar.

1 Using your mouse, highlight the contents of the Address Bar and delete them.

2 Type find NASA (see **Figure 3-22**). As you type, a menu will drop down below the Address Bar in the way you have seen when using the AutoComplete feature.

3 When you have finished typing, either press [Enter] or click the completed search phrase on the menu that has appeared below the Address Bar.

4 Internet Explorer will open the Search Explorer Bar to MSN Autosearch and automatically load its top search result into the browser window (see **Figure 3-23**). In this case, the top result is NASA's home page at www.nasa.org. Other search results are listed in the Explorer Bar.

5 Close the Search Explorer Bar.

More

As you can see, this is a comparatively "plain vanilla" way to search the Web – which means it's great if you want to check something quickly, but not necessarily the best way to start a detailed search of a complicated topic. Another advantage it offers is that you can start your search without first opening the Search Assistant or another page, which means it's a timesaver. And it can be a great way to impress your friends with your Web savvy.

You can control how the Autosearch feature operates from the Customize Search Settings window. If you click the Autosearch settings button at the bottom of the window, the Customize Autosearch Settings (see **Figure 3-24**) window will appear. From this window, you can choose which search service will be used for Address Bar searches, and how the browser window will behave when a search is initiated.

Figure 3-22 Entering an Autosearch query

Figure 3-23 Results of search with MSN Autosearch

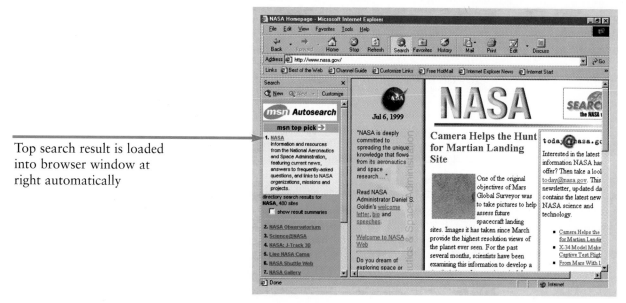

Top search result is loaded into browser window at right automatically

Figure 3-24 Customize Autosearch Settings window

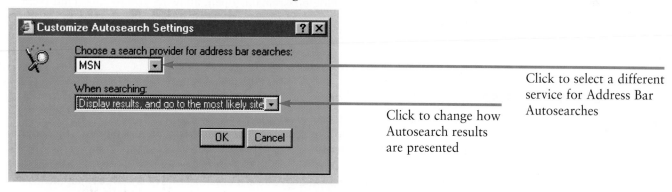

Click to select a different service for Address Bar Autosearches

Click to change how Autosearch results are presented

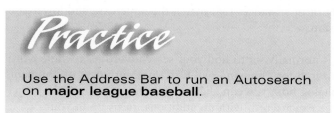

Use the Address Bar to run an Autosearch on **major league baseball**.

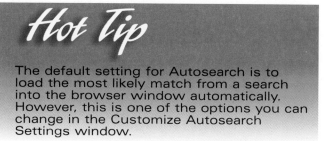

The default setting for Autosearch is to load the most likely match from a search into the browser window automatically. However, this is one of the options you can change in the Customize Autosearch Settings window.

Searching on the Current Page

Concept

By now you know how vast the Web is, and you have come to appreciate the value of search engines. But what about individual Web pages themselves? Some of them are pretty vast, too. Often, when you find the page that contains the information you are looking for, the page is so voluminous that your search hardly feels like it is over. Internet Explorer allows you to search for text within a displayed Web page, using a feature that will look familiar to many users of popular word processors.

Do It!

Find a phrase in the journals of Lewis and Clark.

1 Go to the page www.pbs.org/lewisandclark/archive.

2 Click the link for The Journals and scroll to the bottom of the page that loads. Without changing any of the options at the bottom of the page, click Submit. If this resource on the PBS Web site is no longer available, find another Web page with a large amount of text on it.

3 When the new page has loaded, click Edit on the menu bar and then click Find (on This Page) (see **Figure 3-25**).

4 A dialog box appears that is similar to the Find function in a word processor. In the Find what: text box, type the word human.

5 Click the Find Next button as shown in **Figure 3-26**.

6 Internet Explorer will find and highlight the word human on the page in Sergeant Patrick Gass's May 14, 1804 journal entry describing the unknown road ahead (see **Figure 3-27**). The Find dialog box remains open, allowing you to click Find Next again if you want to search for later occurrences of the same text string in this document. In this example there no further occurrences.

7 Close the Find dialog box.

More

Note that the Find dialog box gives you a selection of useful options. By clicking radio buttons you can elect to search down, or forward, in a document (the default setting), or up, (backward).

The default settings for a Find also allow a case-insensitive search, which means that capital letters do not matter, and a search for "human" will find an occurrence of "Human." However, you can click the box for Match case to specify that Internet Explorer find only those instances that match the uppercase and lowercase usage in your search criterion.

Finally, Internet Explorer is normally set to find your search word as a whole word or as a word fragment: a search for "human" will turn up occurrences of "humanity" or "humane." In the dialog box, you can click the box for Match whole word only to specify that only the exact word, with no additions, turns up in your search.

Figure 3-25 Activating the Find command

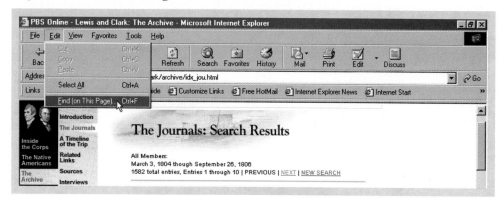

Figure 3-26 Find dialog box

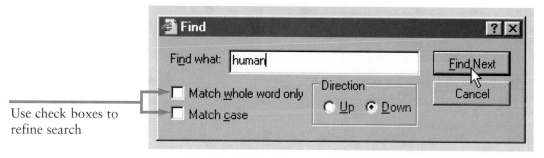

Use check boxes to
refine search

Figure 3-27 Successful search with Find command

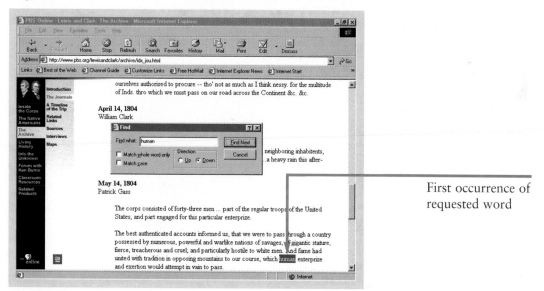

First occurrence of
requested word

Practice

Use the PBS site to find the Lewis and
Clark expedition's journal entries for
November 7, 1805 and find the word **joy**.

Hot Tip

Try to make your search words unique. If
you are searching the **Declaration of
Independence** and want to find the phrase
"When in the course of human events,"
search for "course," not "the," since there
are lots of "the's" in the document.

Shortcuts

Function	Button/Mouse	Menu	Keyboard
Activate Search Explorer Bar	[search icon]	Click View, highlight Explorer Bar, then click Search	[Ctrl]+[E]
Find text on current page		Click Edit, then click Find (on This Page)	[Ctrl]+[F]
Begin new search in Search Explorer Bar	New		[Alt]+[N]
Run same search with next search engine	Next		[Alt]+[X]
Customize search settings	Customize		[Alt]+[Z]

Identify Key Features

State the names, and where applicable, the functions of the items indicated by callouts in **Figure 3-28**.

Figure 3-28 Elements of searching with Internet Explorer

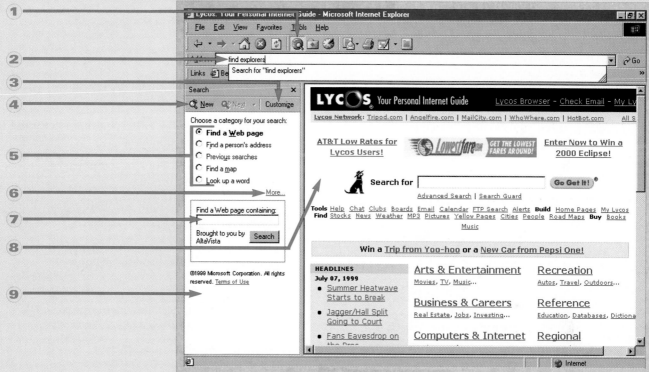

Select The Best Answer

10. The process of finding previously unknown Web pages based on keywords

11. An electronic bulletin board on a specific topic of interest

12. A Web site that lets you find other Web sites relevant to a topic or question

13. The links to relevant pages that appear after a successful search

14. A word that can be used to search quickly from the Address Bar

15. A particular kind of search that is organized specially under the Search Assistant

16. A list of links from a search that you have recalled after moving on to something else

17. The menu item that lets you locate a coword or text string on the current page

18. A feature of Internet Explorer that organizes, manages, and saves your searches

a. Category

b. Find

c. Go

d. Newsgroup

e. Previous search

f. Results list

g. Search

h. Search Assistant

i. Search engine

Quiz (continued)

Complete the Statement

19. A Web search cannot help you locate:

    a. Web pages

    b. People's addresses

    c. Your current location

    d. A map of your current location

20. You can customize the Search Assistant in all these ways except:

    a. Always using your favorite search site

    b. Deactivating the Find a Map category

    c. Always using your favorite search site first

    d. Finding your search keyword only when it appears in all uppercase letters

21. "Relevance" describes:

    a. How closely a Web page relates to your search topic

    b. How important the topic of your search is

    c. How much the page you locate resembles the page you just left

    d. How out-of-date the information is on the page you have found

22. When you save Search results and recall them later, you can:

    a. See if any new information on your topic has been added to the Web

    b. Look at a Web page whose link you did not follow the first time

    c. See how changes you have made to the Search Assistant altered the results

    d. Check the results of a search you did 20 searches ago

23. To locate a word on the current Web page, use the:

    a. Search Explorer Bar

    b. Search Assistant

    c. Address Bar

    d. Find command

24. If you access a search engine by typing its URL in the Address Bar:

    a. You can look up the pages you find later using the Previous searches function

    b. You will be able to look at found pages without losing your search results

    c. You will be able to look at found pages without losing sight of your search results

    d. You will be able to customize the way the search engine looks in the browser window

25. You can use all of the following terms to start a search from the Address Bar except:

    a. Search

    b. Go

    c. Find

    d. ?

26. You can change the order in which search engines are consulted by the Search Assistant from the:

    a. Address Bar

    b. Customize Autosearch Settings window

    c. Customize Search Settings window

    d. MSN AutoSearch Expedia guide

Interactivity

Test Your Skills

1. Open the Search Assistant and practice searching the Web:

   a. Find a Web page about your favorite sports team, music group or organization.

   b. Look up the address of a friend you haven't seen in years.

   c. Find information on the company you work for, or a company you patronize.

   d. Locate a map of the town where you grew up, then print it out.

2. Customize the Search Assistant:

   a. Change the order of the search categories so that maps come first, then Web pages, then people's addresses, then companies.

   b. Change the available search engines for finding Web pages so that only your three favorite sites are enabled.

3. Go back to a previous search and find a fact you didn't know on a page you didn't look at the first time. Copy the information into a word processor file.

4. Access five or six of the most popular search engines manually by typing their URLs into the Address Bar (remember, nearly all use www.enginename.com):

   a. Conduct the same search on each of them and compare the results you receive.

   b. Note which advanced search options, "search within results" options and other features they all offer.

   c. Look up news headlines on the ones that offer them, and compare the news stories that appear via the different engines.

5. Find a Web site that offers:

   a. Job listings, and find listings for your profession.

   b. Apartment ads, and find vacancies in your community.

   c. Sports scores, and find all the references to your favorite player.

   d. Television listings, and find out what time "I Love Lucy" is on. It's always on somewhere.

Interactivity (continued)

Problem Solving

1. You are a Project Manager for a graphic design company. A friend has suggested that you give your team an afternoon off for a team picnic to increase camaraderie and morale. Use the Search Assistant to find a Web page that lists public parks in your county. Then use the Search Assistant to find a map of the park you have chosen for the picnic, or the neighborhood in which it is located. Then visit the Web page of any search engine, and conduct a search to find out more details about the park.

2. After much trial and error, you have finally figured out which search services give you the best results most often. Customize your Search Assistant settings accordingly:

   a. In the Find a Web page category, use only MSN Web Search, AltaVista, and Yahoo!, in that order.

   b. In the Find a person's address category, use only Bigfoot for both Mailing address and E-mail address.

   c. In the Find a Business category, use all available services, but put them in the same order for Name and Category.

   d. Deactivate the Find a picture category.

3. The human resources department at your company recently hosted a seminar on stress relief for the businessperson. Based on what you learned at the seminar, you have decided to that you need to start a new hobby as a way of escaping the rigors of your work. Conduct an Autosearch from Internet Explorer's Address Bar on hobbies. Explore the links that result from the search and select three different hobbies that interest you. Run searches on the three hobbies themselves.

4. The Internet has played a crucial role in the sheer growth and technological progress of telecommuting. Your consulting firm has been hired by another consulting firm to gather data on the latest trends in telecommuting. You will start your research, appropriately, with the World Wide Web. Use the Search Assistant to find Web pages that discuss telecommuting. Visit each of the links returned in the first set of results. Then, since your research must be exhaustive, run the same search using each of the search engines that the Search Assistant makes available. Print one page of three best sites you find.

L E S S O N

EXPLORING THE WEB

The skills you've learned so far have been your passport into the Web – the tools you need to get in, look around and find what you need. Now, it's time to take off your shoes, get comfortable and start living in the Web – using its higher-level resources, taking advantage of Web site properties to suit your security needs and ethical standards, and making Internet Explorer into a personal reflection of the work you do and the places you go every day.

The first thing we'll do in this section is to explore Favorites, the feature that lets you keep a permanent record of sites you want to revisit and organize them in categories of your own creation. We will also examine a few other ways to keep frequently used URLs on hand.

Recently, the use of audio and video media on the Web has blossomed. Internet Explorer will let you find audio and video files on the Web, access them and play them – but that's not all. With a fast enough Internet connection, you can actually see live audio and hear live video through a real-time process called "streaming."

With more content on the Web, people concerned about offensive material or family access to certain materials grows as well. Internet Explorer has features that allow you to monitor and control what you and your family sees. Another growing concern, as more and more people exchange credit card numbers and other sensitive material over the Web, is security. Internet Explorer contains a way to verify the legitimacy of a Web site when you're doing sensitive work over it.

Internet Explorer and the World Wide Web are both full of surprises, and you should regard the skills you've learned in this text as only a start. By now you have the most important ability for a Web surfer: the ability to pose your own questions and find the answers on your own. You haven't been in every room of the Web yet, but you have the master key.

 # Using Favorites

Concept

Internet Explorer can save the URLs of Web sites you wish to revisit in a permanent location called Favorites. Favorites are Internet shortcuts, and work with an Explorer Bar, like the History and Search functions. Using the Favorites Bar, you can create folders to organize shortcuts to your favorite sites, export them to another application or computer, and even arrange to have sites viewable when you are not online. Overall, using Favorites prevents you from having to remember and enter long URLs each time you want to a visit a particular site.

Do It!

Add a Web page to your list of Favorites.

1. Direct your browser to the National Park Service page, **www.nps.gov**.

2. Click Favorites on the menu bar, then click Add to Favorites (see **Figure 4-1**). The Add Favorite dialog box will appear with the name of the current page.

3. Click ⬜ OK to accept the Favorite with its default settings as in **Figure 4-2**.

4. Click the Home button, or go to any other Web site.

5. Click the Favorites button on the Standard Buttons toolbar (see **Figure 4-3**). The Favorites Explorer Bar will open on the left side of the browser window. The Favorites Bar may include preinstalled folders and favorites, and should also display the Favorite you just added.

6. Click the ParkNet favorite, as shown in **Figure 4-4**. The page will load and appear in the right panel of your browser window.

More

There are two principal advantages of the Favorites function over the History file and saved previous searches. The most important one is that it is permanent: if you visit a lot of pages after the one you like, it will be dropped from your History file, and only 10 previous searches remain on file. A site you have saved as a Favorite is there until you decide to delete it.

The other advantage is that you can organize your Favorites. For example, if you visit the National Park Service site and check out seven or eight different parks, you can create a folder within Favorites called "National Parks" and save the individual park pages in there. Then, if you visit a half-dozen sites about baseball, you can create a "Baseball" folder and save those pages there. This makes it more convenient to look up a site you have saved.

As you saw in the example above, Favorites has a few folders already established the first time you use it. These contain sites that the creators of Internet Explorer thought you might find useful. If your computer came loaded with Internet Explorer right out of the box, it may have a preloaded Favorites folder containing sites that your computer's manufacturer thought you would like to see.

Figure 4-1 Adding a Favorite

Figure 4-2 Add Favorite dialog box

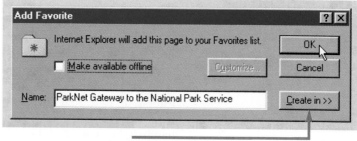

Click here to create Favorite in
a location other than the main
level of the Favorties folder

Internet Explorer 5.0

Figure 4-4 Opening a Favorite

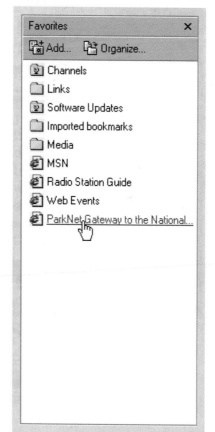

Figure 4-3 Opening the Favorites Explorer Bar

Practice

Visit **www.altavista.com** and add the
page to your Favorites list. Then visit
another page and return to AltaVista using
the Favorite you just created.

Hot Tip

Your Favorites are also listed on the menu
bar's Favorites menu, so you can access
them without activating the Favorites
Explorer Bar.

Organizing Favorites

Concept

Because it does not expire after time (like History) or use (like previous searches), your list of Favorites can grow significantly. If you are headed for a ski weekend and save the resort's Web site so you can look at the snow report during the week leading up to it, that URL will remain in your Favorites folder until you deliberately remove it. There is also the matter of variety: suppose you are really interested in baseball, but you also like sailing, paintball, Delta blues music and theories about Sasquatch. If you threw in a few news and weather sites and kept it all as one big list, it would be a scrambled mess.

To solve this problem, Internet Explorer lets you create folders and organize your individual Favorites in them, much in the same way that you use folders to organize your word processing documents, spreadsheets and other files. You can create and delete folders, decide what goes in them, and even have folders within folders.

Do It!

Create a folder for a certain topic within Favorites and move an existing Favorite into the new folder.

1. Click Favorites on the menu bar, then click Organize Favorites, as in **Figure 4-5**. The Organize Favorites dialog box, shown in **Figure 4-6**, appears.

2. Click the Create Folder button [Create Folder]. A new folder will appear in the list to the right with the default name New Folder highlighted.

3. Type National Parks to replace the highlighted default name.

4. Press [Enter] to confirm the new folder name. The dialog box should now resemble **Figure 4-7**.

Figure 4-5 Organize Favorites command

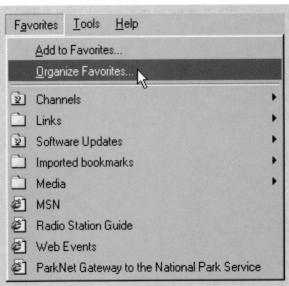

Figure 4-6 Organize Favorites dialog box

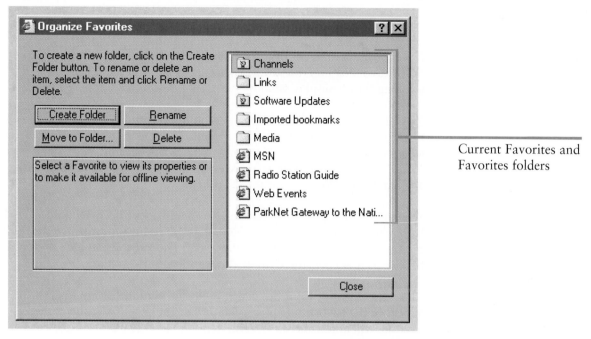

Current Favorites and
Favorites folders

Figure 4-7 New Favorites folder

Properties of
selected Favorite

Folder just created

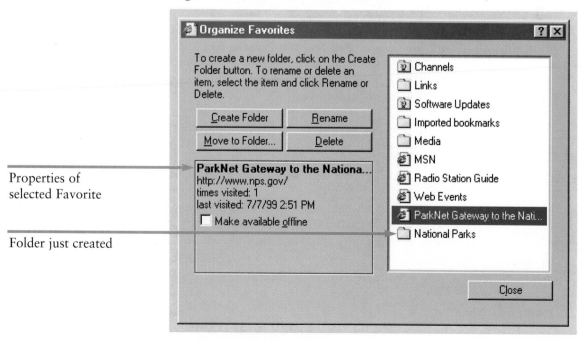

Organizing Favorites (continued)

Do It!

5 Place the mouse pointer over the icon for the ParkNet Favorite inside the Organize Favorites dialog box (the titles of your Favorites will often be truncated if they are too long for the display window).

6 Press down the left mouse button and hold it down as you drag the mouse pointer toward the National Parks folder. A faint representation of the Favorite name and icon will travel along with the mouse pointer as you drag it (see **Figure 4-8**). The mouse pointer will appear as a circle with a line through it as long as it is not over an eligible drop location for the Favorite.

7 When the mouse pointer is over the National Parks folder (the folder will become highlighted), and the standard pointing arrow has reappeared, release the mouse button to drop the Favorite into the folder. The ParkNet favorite disappears from the list, as it is now stored inside the National Parks folder.

8 Close the Organize Favorites dialog box. The National Parks folder will now appear in the Favorites Explorer Bar. If you click the folder there, the ParkNet Favorite will appear below it. Both items are also available on the Favorites menu. See **Figure 4-9** for a representation of the new items in both locations.

More

The method described above allows you to organize Favorites you have already created, even when you are not looking at the pages in question or not even online. It does not let you create new Favorites as you did in the last skill lesson. However, you may have noticed that the Add Favorite dialog box you used in the last skill offers you many of the same organizational options as the Organize Favorites dialog box you just used. You can use this option to organize a Favorite at the same time you save it. The Add Favorite box appears in truncated form the first time you use it, but if you click the Create In button, the full-scale version (see **Figure 4-10**) gives you the chance to create new folders and select the folder in which the new Favorite will be created.

If dragging Favorites in the Organize Favorites dialog box is giving you difficulty, click the Move to Folder button. This will open the Browse for Folder dialog box, which allows you to select a destination folder for the favorite you are moving and actually move it with a series of simple clicks.

You can also add and organize Favorites by clicking the appropriate buttons at the top of the Favorites Explorer Bar.

Figure 4-8 Moving a Favorite

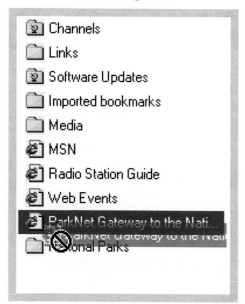

Figure 4-9 Updated Favorites Bar and menu

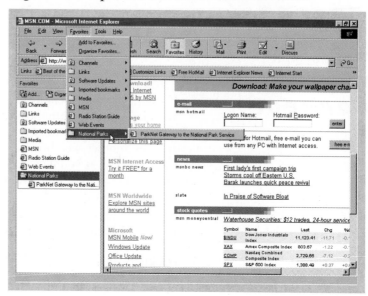

Internet Explorer 5.0

Figure 4-10 Expanded Add Favorite dialog box

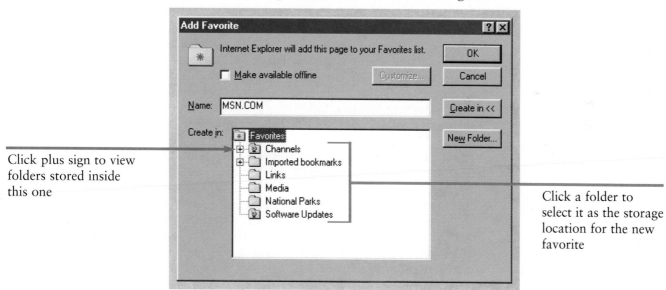

Click plus sign to view folders stored inside this one

Click a folder to select it as the storage location for the new favorite

Practice

Create Favorites folders for some of the other types of Web sites you have visited so far, such as History and Search Engines. Then move any favorites you have created into the appropriate folder.

Hot Tip

In the Organize Folders box, you can create a folder and then drag it into another folder, giving you multiple layers of organization. For example, you could have folders inside the National Parks folder titled "Rockies," "Maritime," "Appalachian," and so forth.

Sharing Favorites

Concept

If you have thought enough of a certain set of Web pages to save them as Favorites, you may want to share them with someone else. Or you may wish to send them – or, export them – to another file or application, such as a presentation you are creating or another Web browser you also use. Internet Explorer lets you take Favorites folders you have marked and export them to your hard drive, where you save them in a location of your choosing and can use them just like any other file.

Do It!

Export a Favorites folder for use in an e-mail message to a friend.

1. Click File, then click Import and Export. This will launch the Import/Export Wizard, shown in **Figure 4-11**. A wizard is a series of specialized dialog boxes designed to help you complete a task one step at a time.

2. Read the introductory screen and then click [Next >] to advance to the next step.

3. On the second screen, click Export Favorites to select it in the list of action choices, and then click Next.

4. On the third screen, click the National Parks folder to select it as the folder you want to export.

5. Advance to the fourth screen (see **Figure 4-12**), from which you determine where to export the folder. Click the radio button labeled Export to a File or Address. To accept the default file location, click Next. Otherwise, click the Browse button to select a different location. Either way, be sure to remember this location, as you will need to know it to access the Favorites file.

6. The last step of the Wizard confirms that you are ready to complete your task. Click the Finish button [Finish]. Your folder of Favorites will be saved in the indicated location as an HTML file. A small dialog box will appear to confirm that the operation was completed successfully. When you compose your e-mail message, you can use your e-mail application's "attach," "enclose," or similar function to take that file and append it to your message. You can use a similar process to bring the folder into a word processing document, a presentation creation application, or another Web browser.

More

This function allows you to export the entire Favorites folder if you wish. If you remember, when you reached the step in the Wizard where you selected the National Parks folder, the screen appeared with Favorites selected at the top of the list. To export your entire Favorites folder, simply leave it selected and continue with the Wizard. This feature is extemely helpful if you have decided to change browsers but do not want to lose shortcuts to all of your favorite sites.

Figure 4-11 Introduction to the Import/Export Wizard

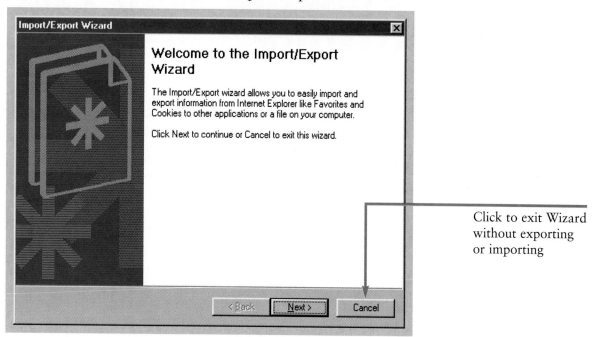

Click to exit Wizard without exporting or importing

Figure 4-12 Choosing a destination

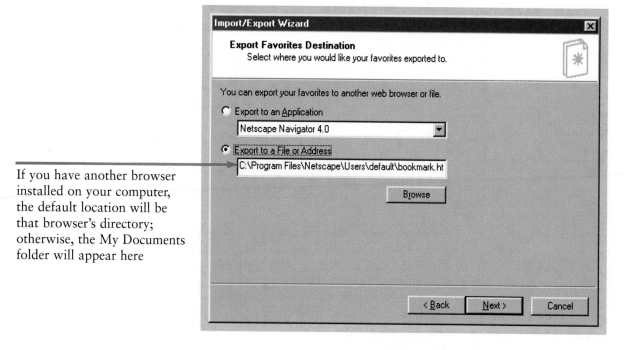

If you have another browser installed on your computer, the default location will be that browser's directory; otherwise, the My Documents folder will appear here

Practice

Export one of the Favorites folders you created in the previous Practice to your hard drive.

Hot Tip

The saved folder full of Favorites contains only the sites' URLs, not their whole content, so it will be comparatively small, and therefore much easier to download if you e-mail it to a friend.

 **Viewing Web Pages Offline**

Concept

Earlier you learned how to save entire Web pages as files in your computer, which is one way to view them when you are not connected to the Internet. Internet Explorer offers a more automated way to "harvest" selected pages from the Web for you to view later. Depending upon the settings you specify, it will download a selected page on a schedule you set, or only when you give a command before logging off. You can save only the page itself, or you can have Internet Explorer follow links on the page as many "levels" down as you wish and save those pages as well. You can even request to receive e-mail notification when a page's contents have changed.

Using this function, you can set Internet Explorer to download the sports page, for example, or the weather, without taking the time to read them while you are online. Then you will be able to read those pages later, and even follow links on them if you have saved more than one level deep. This can be a great cost-cutting measure if you pay for your Internet access hourly, or have an access number that is not a local call. If you have used earlier versions of Internet Explorer, you may know this feature by its old name Subscriptions.

Do It!

Make a Web page you have saved as a Favorite available for offline viewing.

1. On the menu bar, click Favorites and then click Organize Favorites.

2. In the Organize Favorites dialog box that opens, click the National Parks folder to reveal its contents, and then click the ParkNet favorite to select it.

3. Click the Make available offline check box that has appeared to place a check mark in it, as in **Figure 4-13**.

4. A button labeled Properties will appear. Click the button to open the Properties dialog box for the Web page.

5. Click the Schedule tab to bring it forward as seen in **Figure 4-14**. If you wanted to set a schedule for Internet Explorer to download the contents of your page from the Web, you would click the radio button labeled Using the following schedule(s): and click the Add button to open the New Schedule dialog box shown in **Figure 4-15**. In this box, you would set the interval of days and time of day (the present time is the default) and give that schedule a name; back on the Schedule tab you just left, the white area that is empty now would contain a menu of schedules you created. Of course, Internet Explorer would only perform these scheduled downloads if your Internet connection was active at the specified time. For the purposes of this exercise, leave the radio button labeled Only when I choose Synchronize from the Tools menu selected.

Figure 4-13 Marking a favorite for offline viewing

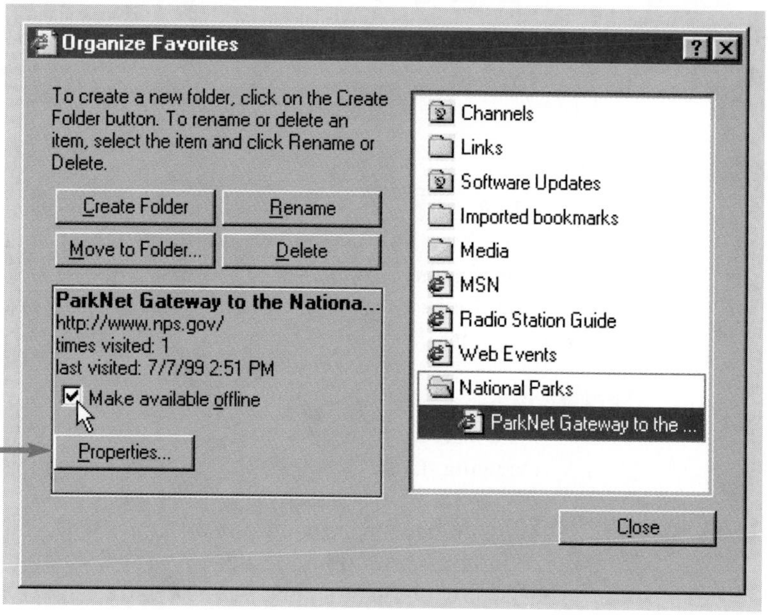

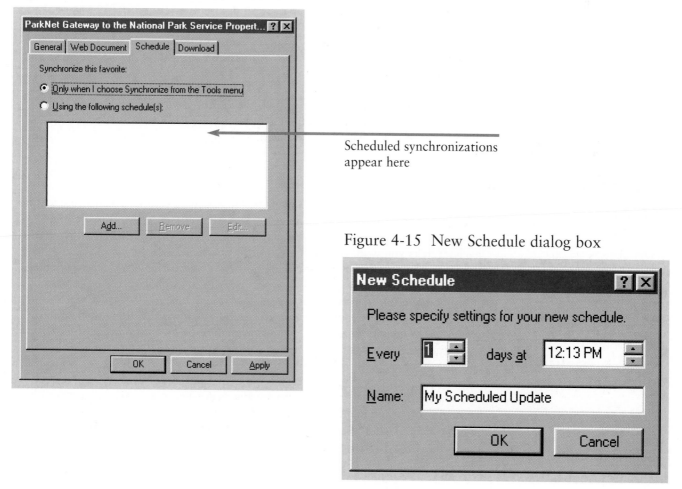

Click to set schedule
for downloading

Figure 4-14 Schedule tab for selected favorite

Scheduled synchronizations
appear here

Figure 4-15 New Schedule dialog box

Viewing Web Pages Offline (continued)

Do It!

6 Click [OK] to close the Properties dialog box, and then close the Organize Favorites box to save your settings. Depending on how your browser is configured, the Synchronizing dialog box may appear, and the Web page will be downloaded for the first time. This process may take several minutes. When the download is complete, close the dialog box.

7 When you are done browsing the Web and ready to close your Internet connection, you will want to download the latest version of a page you have set for offline viewing. Click Tools on the menu bar, then click Synchronize. A dialog box titled Items to Synchronize will appear, as in **Figure 4-16**, that lists the pages you have set for offline viewing and, possibly Internet Explorer Channels that provide special content from a number of well-known companies. You can use this dialog box to select which pages and channels will be synchronized. When only the pages you want to download this time have check marks in the boxes next to them, click the Synchronize button [Synchronize] to proceed.

8 Internet Explorer will download the current contents of the pages you have set for offline viewing, without displaying them in the browser window (see **Figure 4-17**). When the process is completed, you may sever your Internet connection and even exit Internet Explorer or power down your computer without losing the Web pages you have downloaded.

9 To a view a Web page offline, open Internet Explorer without activating your Internet connection. Then open the Favorites Explorer Bar or Favorites menu and click the favorite for the page you downloaded in the last operation. It will load from your hard disk as though it were being loaded from the Web.

More

In the Properties dialog box that opens for a particular favorite when you click the Properties button in the Organize Favorites dialog box, click the Download tab to explore the features offered there. Using these options, you can specify how many levels of links you want Internet Explorer to download when it synchronizes a page. You can set a limit on how much hard disk space a downloaded page may occupy, which will come in handy if your favorite site usually contains, say, tour info on a band but one day suddenly includes a few megabytes of pictures and song lyrics. You can specify that you want to receive e-mail notification when a page changes its contents. Finally, for pages that require password authorization to view, you can enter your password so that it will be transmitted automatically for purposes of the download.

Remember that when you view pages in this mode, you are only reading material from your own computer's hard disk, and cannot receive new content unless you connect to the Web and reload the page. If you set a news page for offline viewing and Synchronize (download) it on Tuesday, then turn your computer on and view it Friday, you'll still see Tuesday's news.

Figure 4-16 Preparing to synchronize

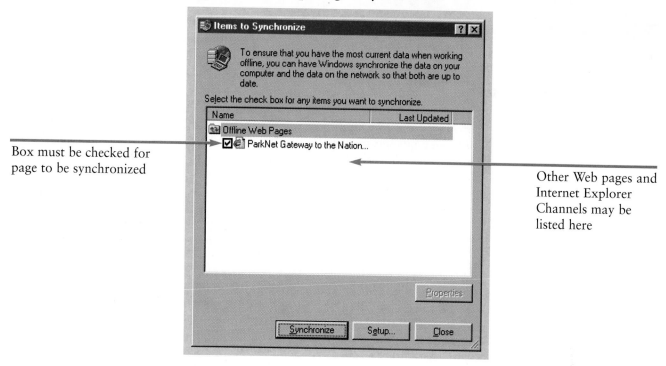

Box must be checked for
page to be synchronized

Other Web pages and
Internet Explorer
Channels may be
listed here

Figure 4-17 Synchronizing Web pages

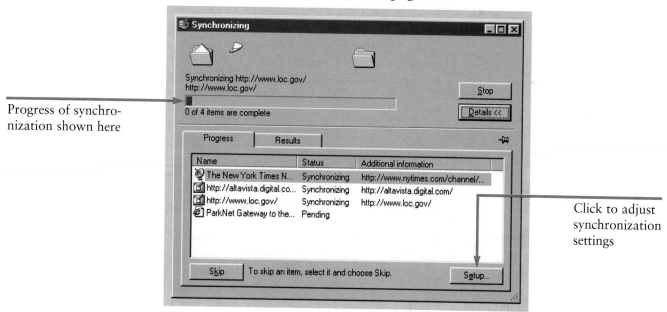

Progress of synchro-
nization shown here

Click to adjust
synchronization
settings

Practice

Add a Web page to your Favorites list and
set it for offline viewing. Then synchronize
the page and view it after you close your
Internet connection.

Hot Tip

Users of Windows 98 can access their
Favorites folder from the Start menu.
Internet Explorer will launch automatically
when you open a favorite in this manner.

Internet Explorer 5.0

Using the Links Toolbar

Concept

The Links toolbar is component of the Favorites folder that has a unique display area. It is a place where you can store the very few URLs that you visit so frequently, even a quick trip to the Favorites Explorer Bar is too much of a detour. There are a variety of very intuitive ways to add a site to your Links toolbar, and once you have done it, that site will appear as a button that gives you one-click access to the page it represents.

Do It!

Create a button on the Links toolbar for a Web page you visit frequently.

1 If you do not see the Links toolbar at all, click View on the menu bar, highlight Toolbars, and then click Links on the submenu. If your Links toolbar appears only as a small tab at the end of the Address Bar, place the mouse pointer over it and drag it downward, releasing the mouse button when the extended Links toolbar appears below the Address Bar. As you can see, the Links toolbar comes with several buttons already added. Those that do not fit on the main bar appear on a menu that can be opened by clicking the double arrow at the right end of the toolbar.

2 Use whatever method you choose to go to the National Park Service home page.

3 In the Address Bar, click and hold your mouse button on the icon next to the URL http://www.nps.gov. Drag the icon toward the Links toolbar. Notice that as you first begin to drag it, the mouse pointer will acquire a gray rectangle and a shortcut icon. Once you reach the Links toolbar, the pointer will appear either as a circle with a line through it (indicating you cannot drop the item there) or with a bold I-beam shaped marker (indicating where the item will go if you drop it just then), as in **Figure 4-18**.

4 Keep dragging the mouse pointer along the toolbar until the marker appears in front of the third link, in this case Customize Links, and release the mouse button. The new shortcut button will appear, as shown in **Figure 4-19**. From now on, you will be able to call up the National Park Service page merely by clicking the button you have created for it on the Links toolbar.

More

If you right-click a button on the Links Bar, a pop-up menu appears that will let you perform many of the operations we have learned: sending the link to someone, setting it for offline viewing, printing it or viewing its properties. You can also rename it or delete it entirely. In the same way you dragged a URL from the Address Bar to the Links toolbar to create a new Link, you can drag a URL from the Favorites Explorer Bar. You can even drag a link from a Web page onto the Links toolbar to make it into a Links button! Remember when dragging URLs around to depress your mouse button and drag without letting go. If you give a URL, a Favorite, or an online link the old traditional "click and release," you won't drag the URL – you will just open the page. If you prefer not to use the Links toolbar often, you may wish to drag it back to its former, reduced location next to the Address Bar, or anywhere else you wish. You can also turn it off completely from the View menu by clicking its name on the Toolbars submenu.

Figure 4-18 Creating a shortcut button on Links toolbar

Indicates where new button will appear

Indicates that an item is being dragged

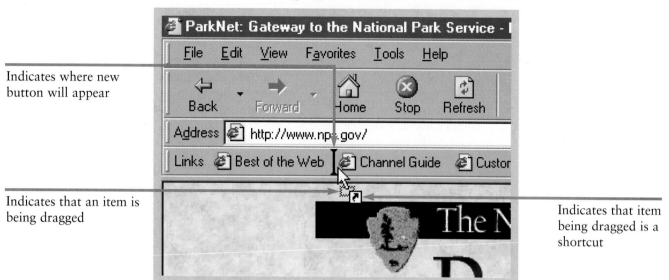

Indicates that item being dragged is a shortcut

Figure 4-19 New Links toolbar button

ScreenTip provides basic properties when you point to button

Practice

Visit the Web page of your favorite search engine and create a button for it on the Links toolbar.

Hot Tip

Only the top few sites you use all the time belong on the Links toolbar; if you include too many sites there, it will grow too big to be convenient. To use an analogy, think of Favorites as your phone directory and Links as your speed dial.

Using Audio Files on the Web

Concept

Just as a Web page can contain text, pictures, and links to other sites, it can contain sound files that your computer can play. Some Web pages contain sounds or background music that plays without any commands from you. Most of the Web's audio content, however, is in the form of files you choose to open. This is in part because the files can be quite large and the page author does not want to make you waste download time on something you do not explicitly want to hear.

Some sound files can be opened and heard using software that you already have as part of your Windows operating system. However, you should know that many sound files on the Web use formats prescribed by other applications not connected to Microsoft or Internet Explorer, which are usually available free (often right alongside the sound files themselves). The most common of these applications is a product called the RealPlayer. If a file you want to hear requires that you download and use this or a similar product, you will find the instructions easy to follow and the controls simple and intuitive. Of course, your computer must have properly connected speakers, either built in or peripheral, for you to hear sound files on the Web.

Do It!

Access and listen to a sound file you receive over the Web.

1. Go to the National Public Radio Web site, www.npr.org. At the top of the page, there are several options for "Listen to the latest news." Click Windows Media, which will allow you to hear the audio content using Windows Media Player, a piece of software that is probably already on your computer. You must have an Internet connection that can handle the speeds indicated.

2. When you have clicked the Windows Media option, you will likely see a page offering to help you download Windows Media Player. Before you go ahead with any download, go to the bottom of the page and click the This Hour's Newscast link – that is, bypass the download option, because you probably already have Windows Media Player. If it does not work and you do not have the player, you can always go back and follow the instructions to perform the download.

3. Windows Media Player will open as in **Figure 4-20**. At first, it will appear as if the dancing Windows logo in the player's screen is the only thing happening, but at the bottom of the player window you will notice a status bar that is tracking the opening of the audio file. Since these files are often large, it may take a few moments. When the file (or an initial segment of it) has loaded, the player window's display screen will disappear and the window will become smaller as in **Figure 4-21**; this is because Media Player, which can handle both audio and video, has recognized that there is no video content to display.

4. The audio will begin to play over your computer's speakers. You can use the stereo-style buttons near the top of the player window to control the playback. There is also a volume control, which you may elect to use instead of any manual volume control on your computer's speakers.

More

Note that the Media Player (or whichever program you use) is not another Web page, but a window that opens separately from Internet Explorer. If you are going to listen to more than one sound file, you can leave the application's window open until you have finished the last one. If you move on to another activity on or off the Web, the window will remain open until you close it. Even if you exit Internet Explorer, any audio content loaded into memory will still be there as long as the player window is active, and you will be able to replay the file. Often, a large sound file will load in segments instead of all at once, a process known as buffering. You will see the player application's status bar fill, then go back to empty, and cycle again. Sometimes during this process, if the data is downloading too slowly, the replay of your file may be interrupted. If you use the RealPlayer instead of Windows Media Player, you will notice that it has a "channels" feature that takes you to some popular sites on the Web that contain audio content. These are not presented by Internet Explorer, but you may choose to explore them as you wish.

Internet Explorer 5.0

Figure 4-20 Windows Media Player

Figure 4-21 Playing an audio file

Practice

Go back to the NPR page and listen to a few more of the available audio files.

Hot Tip

Sometimes IE will ask whether you want to save a file to disk or simply open it (load it into your computer's memory without writing it to a storage device). If you have any doubts about the safety of the site you are visiting, you may wish to select the latter.

Using Video Files on the Web

Concept

Now you are getting to the exciting parts of the Web. Chances are you have tried this already, possibly within the first five minutes after you launched Internet Explorer for the first time. The Web's ability to bring full-motion video, with sound, onto your computer screen is one of its most popular and rapidly growing abilities. Like audio, watching video over the Web requires a special program such as Windows Media Player. If you attempt to play a video without having such a program, you will usually be prompted to download it.

Do It!

View a video file you receive over the Web.

1 Go to www.cnn.com and click the Video link near the top of the page.

2 The page that appears will give you the option of viewing Windows Media video or Real video. Select the Windows Media option that corresponds to your connection speed (if you are unsure of your connection speed, choose 28.8+).

3 Click the link for any story that appears on the page. In this example, Windows Media Player does not open as a separate window; rather, it is launched as a "built-in" part of the page you are viewing (see **Figure 4-22**). You will see it operate both ways as you browse the Web.

4 After what may be a significant download time, the video newscast begins to play.

More

As you can see, the excitement of online video can wear off pretty soon after you view your first small, slow, grainy offering. However, this is one area of the Web that is rapidly improving in quality. Remember that a "video" file almost always means "audio and video," so make sure you have speakers properly connected to your computer.

As you noticed in the last two skill lessons, large audio and video files sometimes download in "chunks" by a process known as buffering: part of the file is transmitted, then played, then another part is transmitted, and if everything goes well, your file runs all the way to the end with no interruptions. Well, what if there were no end? What if the "chunks" never stopped coming?

"Streaming" audio and video works just this way, allowing you not only to receive large media files without waiting for the whole thing to load (if it will fit in your computer's memory at all), but also making live Web broadcasts possible. This process has become especially popular as a way to tune in distant radio stations, since they aren't usually available over networks the way television shows are, and since the audio data is less voluminous than full video. But streaming video is a reality as well, and advances in the Web's transmission ability are certain to make both more commonplace. Listening to radio stations in this way can be one of the most enjoyable experiences on the Web, especially since the broadcast can be left running in the background while you do other work. Make sure you know the bandwidth of your Internet connection, especially if you are at work and sharing a connection. Without knowing it, you may take up so much of the bandwidth with your streaming broadcast that no one else can get any work done.

Most streaming content can be played over the Web using either RealPlayer or Windows Media Player. Internet Explorer simplifies the process of finding Windows Media Player content by providing the Radio toolbar, which you can activate using the View menu's Toolbars command. The Radio toolbar contains a link to Microsoft's Radion Station Guide. It also offers playback controls and the ability to add radio stations to your Favorites list.

Figure 4-22 Playing video on a Web page

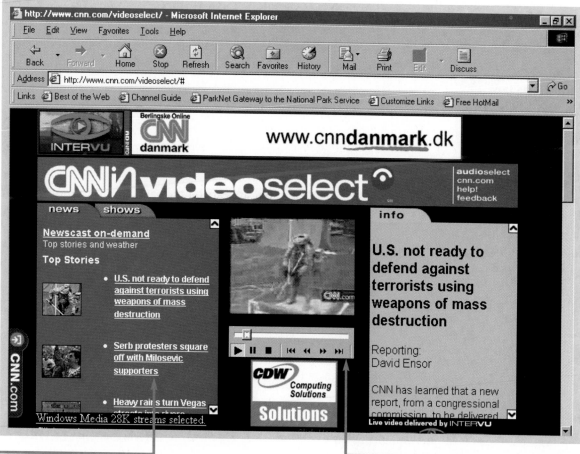

Links to video news stories

Windows Media Player embedded in Web page – still requires that you have the program installed

Practice

Check out video offerings at popular sites like **cnn.org**, **c-span.org**, and **msnbc.com**.

Hot Tip

Downloading video files from the Web demands a lot of "bandwidth," or transmission capacity. Before you start playing video, you may want to make sure any other applications operating over your Internet connection are idle.

Shortcuts

Function	Button/Mouse	Menu	Keyboard
Open Favorites Explorer Bar	🔲	Click View, highlight Explorer Bar, then click Favorites	[Ctrl]+[I]
Add current page to Favorites	Add...	Click Favorites, then click Add to Favorites	[Ctrl]+[D]
Open Organize Favorites dialog box	Organize...	Click Favorites, then click Organize Favorites	[Ctrl]+[B]
Move selected item up in Favorites list in Organize Favorites dialog box	Click and drag		[Alt]+[Up Arrow]
Move selected item down in Favorites list in Organize Favorites dialog box	Click and drag		[Alt]+[Down Arrow]

Identify Key Features

Name the items, and where applicable, identify the function of, the items indicated by callouts in **Figure 4-23**.

Figure 4-23 Advanced browsing items

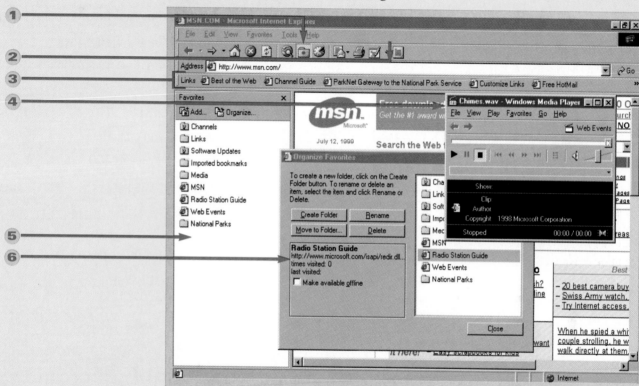

Select The Best Answer

7. Feature that lets you quickly recall your most frequently visited sites

8. An application that allows you to view audio and video material from the Web

9. A way to look at Web pages when your Internet connection is not active

10. The process of retrieving an audio file from the Web then playing it

11. A feature that lets you save and categorize Web sites you visit frequently

12. The process of receiving live audio broadcasts in continuous segments

a. Downloading

b. Windows Media Player

c. Streaming

d. Favorites

e. Offline viewing

f. Organize Favorites

Quiz (continued)

Complete the Statement

13. If you visit a particular Web page every day, you might want to access it as:

    a. A Favorite

    b. A Links toolbar button

    c. Your home page

    d. All of the above

14. The folders you create in Favorites are organized by:

    a. How much you trust the validity of a site

    b. Any distinctions you want to create

    c. How appropriate you feel the site is for kids

    d. How often you view each site in the folder

15. The most accurate description of viewing sites offline is that:

    a. It lets you get the latest news updates when you cannot get to your Internet connection

    b. It lets you save a page for later so you can follow links from it to the rest of the Web

    c. It is automatically available for any page you viewed during your last online browsing session

    d. It provides a snapshot of a page's contents as of the last time you were online

16. The Links toolbar is:

    a. A permanent fixture on the screen

    b. Located under the Start menu

    c. Part of your Favorites hierarchy

    d. An Explorer Bar

17. When you send Favorites to another person, the recipient:

    a. Can view them without typing a URL

    b. Can view them without an Internet connection

    c. Can view them without a Web browser

    d. Can view them without worrying about security

18. A Favorite can be created in:

    a. A new folder that you create

    b. The main level Favorites folder

    c. An existing Favorites folder

    d. All of the above

19. The process of Downloading a favorite for offline viewing is called:

    a. Synchronicity

    b. Syncopation

    c. Synchronization

    d. Organization

20. You can access a Microsoft list of streaming audio broadcasters from the:

    a. Add Favorite dialog box

    b. Radio toolbar

    c. CNN Interactive Web site

    d. RealPlayer

Interactivity

Test Your Skills

1. Pick three general topics that interest you. For each topic, perform an Internet search:

   a. Save at least five Web pages on each topic as Favorites. If appropriate, make one of your selections a page whose content changes frequently, such as a news, sports, financial or weather page.

   b. For at least one of the pages you save in each topic, give the Favorite a name different from the default name the Web author gave it.

   c. Create a folder in Favorites for each of your search topics.

   d. Move each of the pages you have saved into the appropriate folder.

   e. After you have ended your browsing session and exited Internet Explorer, launch it again and use Favorites to revisit the topics you researched.

2. Choose one of the topic folders and send it to a friend via e-mail.

3. From among the pages you just found and saved as Favorites, choose one you think you will want to see especially often. Add it to your Links toolbar.

4. Find an audio file on a Web site you consider trustworthy:

   a. Download it, choosing the option to save it to your hard disk. Note the file size and the time it takes to download.

   b. Play the selection over your computer's speakers.

   c. Repeat the process with a video file.

   d. You may wish to delete these files after the exercise to avoid wasting hard drive space.

   e. Find a live audio broadcast on the Web and tune in. Place the broadcast in your operating system's background while you do other work on a word processor, spreadsheet, or other application.

5. Look through Internet Explorer's Menu Bar and find a function we did not discuss anywhere in this text. Experiment with it and try to learn how it works and what it does!

Interactivity (continued)

Problem Solving

1. As a sales representative, you fit the title of "business traveler" perfectly. Fortunately, the World Wide Web can do wonders for your travel expenses. Various Web sites can now assist you in finding the cheapest air fares and hotel rooms available. Use the skills you have learned so far to find at least three of these sites on the Web. Add each site you find to your Favorites list. Then create a new Favorites folder named Travel Savings and move the favorites you have added into the new folder. Finally, export the new folder to a file on your hard drive named PS4-1.htm.

2. As the Director of Human Resources at a large accounting firm, it is important for you to stay on top of the issues that affect the workforce. Chief among these is health insurance. Your approach to this topic is two-fold. You like to keep one eye on what the insurance companies are saying about themselves, and the other on what the watchdogs are saying about the insurance companies. Use your Web skills to find the Web sites of major health care providers. Store the main pages of these sites in a Favorites folder named Health Care Providers. Then focus your Web search on pages that provide reviews of, or news about, particular health care companies. Organize these pages in a Favorites folder named Health Care Reviews. Select two pages from each folder and set them for offline viewing. Synchronize the pages, close your browser and Internet connection, and read the pages offline.

3. Your department is in the market for a new color laser printer. You have been chosen to research the purchase and recommend a printer to your boss. Use your Web skills to find out as much as you can about four top of the line color laser printers. You should search for the Web sites of companies that actually manufacture and sell the printers as well as independent reviews of printers. When you find a page on a manufacturer's site, save it as a favorite in a folder named Printers. When you find a page that review the performance of a particular printer or printers, save it as a favorite in a folder named Printer Reviews. After studying the four candidates you have found, select the printer that you think will best suit your department's needs (a high output rate, low maintenance, network ready, reliable service program). Create a button for the Web page of the printer you have chosen on the Links toolbar.

4. Go to www.cnn.com and click the Video link near the top of the page. Use Windows Media Player to watch video clips of today's top news stories. Then return to CNN's home page and click the Audio link. On the AudioSelect page, listen to a streaming broadcast of CNN's live news coverage.

Glossary

A

Accessibility
The degree to which people with disabilities can make use of material on the Web, which Internet Explorer addresses by allowing changes in colors, text sizes and certain controls.

Active
Term used to describe the window in which you are currently working, especially if more than one window is open.

Address
The characters that tell a browser such as Internet Explorer where a particular resource resides on the World Wide Web, including a root, domain, path and filename. Also called a URL (Uniform Resource Locator).

Address Bar
The area in the browser window where you type in a Web site's address or URL, and where the address of the current page is displayed.

AltaVista
A popular commercial search engine.

Animations
Objects that are part of a Web page and which change or move once loaded, often in a continuous loop.

Application
Also known as a program, a piece of software that contains instructions for your computer and allows you to perform tasks. Internet Explorer is an application.

ARPAnet
An acronym for the U.S. Department of Defense's Advanced Research Projects Agency net, the earliest version (circa late 1960s) of what would become known as the Internet.

Audio files
Files in a particular format (such as .wav) that your computer interprets as sounds using a media player application.

Author
The person or agency who created a Web page.

AutoComplete
A feature of Internet Explorer that remembers entries you have made previously in the Address Bar or other locations and finishes your typing for you when you begin to make the same entry again.

AutoScan
Part of the way in which Internet Explorer can search the Web after a URL you enter has failed; it looks for sites that have the same root you entered but different common domains (such as ".org" or ".edu").

B

Back
A Standard Buttons toolbar button that takes you directly to the last page you viewed before coming to the current page.

Background
(1) The area in the browser window "behind" all the text and graphics on a Web page; it can appear blank, or colored, or in a pattern. (2) The part of your computer's memory where open applications or folders reside when others are open and being used.

Bandwidth
A term used to describe the capacity of an Internet connection, usually expressed in kilobytes (K) per second.

Browser
Any application that interprets HyperText Markup Language (HTML) to display Web pages. Internet Explorer is a browser.

Browser window

The segment of Internet Explorer's display where material from the World Wide Web appears for you to read.

Browsing

A common term for reading material on the Web.

Button

A graphical interface feature that functions like a real-life mechanical button when you click on it with your mouse.

C

Cancel

To halt the loading of a page from the Web before it is completed using the Stop button on the Standard Buttons toolbar.

Case-sensitive

Suceptible to mistakes when uppercase or lowercase letters are used in the wrong places. A case-sensitive application will not interpret "Hello" in the same way it interprets "hello."

Category

A certain kind of Web search – for people, for businesses, for maps, etc. – that you can perform using the Search Assistant.

Certificates

Documents appended to Web pages that help verify their authenticity and authorship for security purposes.

Channels

(1) A term for Web pages that you have set for automatic updating and offline viewing. (2) A feature of the popular RealPlayer application that facilitates access to different sources of audio and video material.

Click

To depress the button on your mouse while the mouse pointer is located over a desired item on the screen. Depending on the function, you may click and hold the button, click it and release it, or click and release it twice ("double-clicking").

Client

A computer which is receiving data or running software from another computer.

Client-server model

A way of arranging computer networks in which data or applications reside on one computer, the host, and one or more other computers, the clients, access these resources via a connection to the host.

Clipboard

The part of your computer's memory where items reside after you have cut or copied them for later use.

Close

To shut down a file, application or window so that it is no longer active and no longer appears on your screen.

Content Advisor

A feature of Internet Explorer that uses ratings standards to help users control access to Web pages which contain potentially objectionable material.

Copy

To capture information, often a segment of text, to the Clipboard so it can be used in another place or in a different application.

Current page

The Web page you are viewing at the moment.

Cursor

A mark on your screen, usually a blinking vertical line, that indicates where the next character you type will appear. The mouse pointer is also sometimes called a cursor.

Customize

To alter the appearance or function of one of Internet Explorer's features to your own liking.

D

Default settings

The way in which certain options are set when Internet Explorer is first used and you haven't changed them – for example, your default home page is probably msn.com.

Desktop

The interactive display that fills your whole screen when you're running Windows and there are no folders or applications open.

Desktop icon

An object on the desktop that you can double-click to open a file, folder or application.

Desktop shortcut

A desktop icon you have created for a particular file, folder or application.

Dialog box

A box that opens when an application requires you to make a decision or enter data.

Disk

A mechanical device for storing data. It can be a removable floppy disk, but in current common usage it usually refers to your computer's hard drive.

Document

In Web terminology, a collection of text, graphics, links and layout information that is saved as a file and makes up a Web page. More generally, any file, especially a text or word processing file.

Domain

The three-letter portion of a URL such as .com, .gov, .org, or .edu that indicates what type of entity created the Web page.

Double-clicking

Depressing and releasing your mouse button twice in rapid succesion, usually to open a file or application from its icon. You can modify the speed of your double-clicks on the Windows control panel.

Download

To transfer data from a server or host computer to a client computer.

Drive

Any device that stores data in a mechanical medium, including floppy disk drives, CD-ROM drives, but most commonly used as shorthand for a computer's internal hard disk drive.

E

Electronic mail

Commonly shortened to "e-mail." Messages sent from one computer user to another via the Internet.

Excite!

A popular commercial search engine.

Exit

To shut down an application.

Explorer Bar

An area containing commands and options that appears on the left-hand side of the browser window when using the History, Favorites or Search Assistant features.

Export

To make a file or folder available for use (or "importing") by another application.

F

Favorites

A feature of Internet Explorer that allows you to maintain organized groups of shortcuts to pages you have viewed in the past.

File

Any information stored as a unit on a computer and accessible by one name. A word processing document, a picture or a Web page are examples of items stored as files.

File tab

Part of the graphical arrangement in certain control boxes, such as "Internet Options," that resembles the cut tabs on a manila file folder and allows you to select from among several "pages" of command screens that appear to be piled on top of one another.

Find

(1) In Internet Explorer, a function that allows you to search the current page for a particular string of text. (2) In Windows, a function that allows you to search a drive or network for a certain file, application or folder.

Folder

A group of files stored together and given a group name so they can be moved or referred to all at once.

Formatting

The instructions that determine where text, pictures and other elements appear on a Web page.

Forms
Areas on a Web page in which you enter data that will be reported back to the server; for example, the space in which you enter your credit card number when making a purchase online.

Forward
A Standard Buttons toolbar button that sends you to a page that you have viewed previously but "retreated" from using the Back button.

Frames
A way in which certain Web pages are arranged that divides the browser window into distinct areas that can be scrolled or changed separately from one another.

FTP (File Transfer Protocol)
A method of transferring data files from one computer to another over the Internet.

G

Go
A button next to the Address Bar that instructs Internet Explorer to access the Web page whose URL you have typed.

Graphic
Any photo, image, drawing or other picture included in a Web page.

H

Help
A feature of Internet Explorer that gives you instructions and advice on using the application.

Highlight
To select a segment of text for a particular use by dragging your mouse over it with the button depressed.

History
A feature of Internet Explorer that automatically saves the addresses of pages you've viewed recently so that you can return to them more easily.

Home
A Standard Buttons toolbar button that returns you to your selected home page.

Home page
(1) The Web site you've selected to be the one that appears when you open Internet Explorer. (2) A common term for the main or opening page of a Web site that cointains many pages.

HotBot
A popular commercial search engine.

Hover
To position your mouse pointer over an object. Some hyperlinks and other objects will change color or animate when you hover over them, even though the mouse button is not depressed.

HTML (HyperText Markup Language)
The source code, or programming language, used to create and reproduce Web pages. A browser, such as Internet Explorer, interprets HTML to create the displays you see.

HTTP (HyperText Transfer Protocol)
The standard by which most Web data (pages and otherwise) is transferred between the server and the client computer.

Hyperlink
An object or text segment that has been made into an active "button" which will take you to another Web page when you click on it.

Hypermedia
Words and pictures that are linked to other sites on the Web and will transport you there when you click on them.

Hypertext
Hypermedia that appears as text.

I

Icon
An object on the Windows desktop that represents a file, folder or application. Also, a loosely used term for some objects displayed in Web pages.

Image
A photo, drawing or other graphical representation that is saved a a file and can be included in a Web page.

Infoseek

A popular commercial search engine.

Internet

An extended world-wide computer network that is composed of numerous smaller networks. The World Wide Web is part of the Internet.

Internet connection

The means by which your computer (the client) is connected to a Web or e-mail server, either through a network or by the use of a modem.

Internet Explorer 5

The latest version of Microsoft's Internet Explorer browser application, introduced in 1999. The subject of this book.

Internet Explorer icon

(1) A desktop icon that represents the Internet Explorer application and allows you to open the application with a double-click. (2) The image of the Internet Explorer symbol that appears in the upper right-hand corner of the browser window; when it is animated, the browser is busy seeking or transferring data.

Internet Options

A very useful group of controls, available under "Tools" on the Menu Bar, that allows you to alter the appearance and function of Internet Explorer in many ways.

Internet ratings

Graded descriptions of certain types of content (e.g. violence, foul language) used by the Content Advisor to control access to certain Web sites.

Internet Zone

A Security Zone that includes all material that is not on your own computer and which you have not previously assigned to a different Security Zone.

ISP (Internet Service Provider)

A company, school or other entity that provides access to an Internet server, often for a fee.

Keyword

A term used as the basis for an Internet search.

Launch

To open an application such as Internet Explorer.

Layout

The spatial arrangement of text, pictures and other objects within a Web page.

Link

(1) Noun, a shortened version of the term hyperlink (see hyperlink). (2) Verb, to connect one element of hypermedia to a particular Web address so that it can serve as a hyperlink.

Links Bar

A portion of the browser window that you can set up to contain one-click shortcuts to a few Web sites you view very often.

Load

To download, or transfer data from a server computer to a client computer. When you access a Web page, you are loading it.

Local Intranet Zone

A Security Zone reserved for material that resides on your local network but not on your own computer.

Log off

To terminate your Internet connection, sometimes by sending the server a specific command, often by simply hanging up the phone.

Log on

To establish a connection to an Internet server, often through the use of a password.

Lycos

A popular commercial search engine.

M

Mail

Another term for e-mail.

Maximize

To display a window across your entire screen.

Media Player

A Microsoft application, commonly included along with Windows or available over the Internet, that interprets sound and audio files so that your computer can play them.

Menu

Any grouped list of commands or options.

Menu Bar

The topmost portion of the browser window, containing a list of categories ("File," "Edit," "View," etc.) that you can click on to view a menu of command options.

Microsoft Outlook

An application from Microsoft that handles e-mail, among other functions.

Minimize

To remove a window (containing an active file, folder or application) from the desktop without closing or exiting it. A minimized window is represented as a button on the status bar at the bottom of the Windows display.

Mouse

A pointing device that converts the movement of your hand into movements of a pointer or cursor on the screen, and includes one or more buttons used to actuate graphical controls.

Mouse pointer

The graphical object that indicates what location on the screen the mouse is covering. Typically a small arrow, in many applications it changes to other shapes to indicate available functions in different locations.

MSN Autosearch

The Microsoft service used for searches from the Address Bar.

N

Navigate

To move among the resources World Wide Web by using the controls on your browser.

Netscape

A popular browser application that has the same basic purpose as Internet Explorer.

Network

A group of computers linked together to share data.

Newsgroup

A portion of the Internet apart from e-mail and the Web, consisting of many separate "bulletin boards" on almost any topic imaginable.

Node

One computer on a network.

NSFnet

An intermediate step in the development of the Internet, created by the National Science Foundation in the early 1980s.

O

Object

Any distinct item on a Web page, such as a picture, an icon, or a block of text.

Offline

Not connected to a server computer.

Online

Connected to a server computer.

Open

To launch or activate an application, or to access the contents of a folder or file.

Operating system

The program that determines how your computer receives commands, handles files and applications, and arranges its display. Windows 95 and Windows 98 are operating systems.

Organize

An option available with many of Internet Explorer's features, allowing you to alter the way they appear or operate.

P

Packet

A "bundle" of information sent electronically from one computer to another; the basis of most networking schemes.

Page

(1) The data that fits on your display all at once without scrolling. (2) A single Web document made up of text, pictures, links, and layout information. (3) Casually, an entire Web site, which in fact may be made up of many pages.

Paste

To insert data from the Clipboard into a new location.

Path

The list of folder names that designates where a particular file resides on a drive or server; frequently part of a URL.

Personal certificates

Security documents you can create to substantiate your identity for use in Internet transactions.

Picture

An image stored as a file and included as part of a Web page.

Platform for Internet Content Selection (PICS)

A standard for ratings labels attached to Web content.

Pop-up menu

A group of command options that appears, if available, when the user clicks the right mouse button. This menu usually pertains directly to the object that was clicked.

Previous searches

A category on the Search Assistant that allows you to view the results of searches you have performed recently.

Print

To send a file, picture or other data to a properly connected printer device so that it will be reproduced on paper.

Print Range

A setting in the Print dialog box that determines what portion of a document will be printed.

Printer

A peripheral device that reproduces data from the computer onto paper.

Program

Another term for application, a piece of software that contains instructions for your computer and allows you to perform tasks. Internet Explorer is a program.

Prompt

A message or dialog box that appears when your operating system, an application or a Web site requires you to enter data.

Properties

Taken as a set, the various qualities of a Web page: its name, size, date of creation and other information. You can view a page's properties under the "File" menu.

Protocol

A scheme for transferring data from one computer to another, such as HTTP (HyperText Transfer Protocol) or FTP (File Transfer Protocol).

Q

Quick Launch toolbar

A feature available on Windows 98 that allows you to create buttons at the bottom of your screen to launch applications with a single mouse click.

Quicktime

A popular format for encoding video files that requires a commercially available application to view them.

R

Radio button

A small, circular area you can click to activate options in many dialog boxes. When a radio button has a dot in it, the option it represents is active.

Ratings

Standardized descriptions, made available by private organizations and readable by Internet Explorer's Content Advisor, of the degree of objectionable content in Web pages.

RealAudio Player

A popular, commercially available application that interprets sound and audio files so that your computer can play them.

Recreational Software Advisory Council (RSAC)

The default rating service that Internet Explorer's Content Advisor is set to use

Refresh

A Standard Buttons toolbar button that loads the contents of the current page again from scratch, useful in correcting transmission errors or viewing updated content.

Relevance

A statistical description of how closely a Web page found in a search matches the criteria you entered for the search. Many search engines rank their findings in order of relevance.

Reload

Another term for Refresh.

Restricted Sites

A Security Zone to which you can assign sites you do not trust.

Results

A list of Web pages that a search engine produces in response to a search topic you've entered.

Right-clicking

Depressing the right-hand button on a mouse that is equipped with one (not all are), often to bring up a menu of options that pertains to the object you have clicked.

S

Save

To write data, such as a file or Web page, on to a disk for storage and later use.

Scroll

To manipulate the display, using scroll bars, arrow keys or a wheel mouse, so that the information moves up and down the screen or side to side, and information in the current page or document that was hidden comes into view.

Search

To use a specially designed Web site to locate Web resources on a particular topic or keyword.

Search Assistant

A feature of Internet Explorer that allows you to organize how you search for different kinds of information on the Web, which search resources you use, and in what order.

Search engine

A special Web site, typically a commercial entity, that is used for searching for Web pages that conform to keywords you enter.

Security Zones

Categories you can assign Web pages to based upon where they reside or how much you trust the validity of their content. Each Security Zone can be set with different safeguards against the downloading of material.

Send Link

To create an e-mail message that contains the URL of the current page for the recipient to use. Available under the "File" menu.

Send Page

To create an e-mail message that contains the entire contents of the current page for the recipient to view. Available under the "File" menu.

Server

The computer where Web pages and other data reside so that your computer, the client, can access them via the Internet or a local network.

Session

The time you spend connected to a Web server and working on the Internet.

Show Picture

A command, available by right-clicking, that enables you to display a particular image even though you've set Internet Explorer not to display pictures in general.

Site

A group of Web pages that relate to one another and all reside on the same server under the same root and domain.

Snap

A popular commercial search engine.

Software
A blanket term that describes all applications.

Standard Buttons toolbar
A portion of the browser window that contains several large buttons ("Back," "Forward," "Stop," etc.) that activate Internet Explorer's principal functions.

Start Menu
In Windows 95 and Windows 98, the principal menu you use to control the operating system. Accessible by clicking the Start button in the lower-left corner of the display.

Status bar
The bottom portion of the browser window, which displays which Security Zone the current page is in, the status of your Internet connection, and the function the browser is currently performing (such as "Finding page" or "Done").

Stop
A Standard Buttons toolbar button that halts the download of a page in progress.

Streaming
A way to send audio and video files in a continuous "stream" of small segments. If your Internet connection and your computer are fast enough, the result is an uninterrupted display of the audio or video material.

Submenu
A menu that appears when a menu item is highlighted; for example, on the Start Menu, you can highlight "Programs" to bring up a submenu of available applications.

Subscriptions
The term used to describe offline viewing of Web pages in earlier versions of Internet Explorer.

Supervisor Password
The code word you can establish to limit other people's ability to change your Content Advisor settings.

Surfing
A common term for browsing the Web, especially used to describe extended sessions in which the user follows links wherever his or her interest takes him with no particular plan in mind.

Synchronize
To download the content of pages you've set for offline viewing, an operation usually performed just before disconnecting from the Internet.

T

Target
The Web document that is connected to a particular hyperlink.

Temporary Internet Files
A location in which Internet Explorer saves the content of pages you have visited recently so that they will load more quickly when you return to them.

Text
Any set of alphanumeric characters.

Text string
A particular set of alphanumeric characters that you enter as the basis for a search.

Tip of the Day
An optional feature available through Internet Explorer's Help function that will greet you with a new piece of advice every time you launch the application.

Toggle
(1) To switch back and forth between two open windows or applications. (2) To alter the state of a command option which has only two possible states, such as "on" or "off."

Toolbar
A graphical segment of the Internet Explorer browser window, or of any application, that contains a selection of buttons you can use to activate functions with the click of a mouse.

Trusted Sites
A Security Zone to which you can assign Web sites whose content you trust.

U

URL (Uniform Resource Locator)
The characters that tell a browser such as Internet Explorer where a particular resource resides on the World Wide Web, including a root, domain, path, and file name. It is also called an Address.

W

Wallpaper

In Windows, an image you set up to be diplayed as the background on your desktop. You can capture images from the Web and use them as wallpaper by right-clicking on them.

Webcam

A still or video camera that produces images a Web author sends out over the Internet, often in real time, 24 hours a day.

Webcast

An event such as a concert or press conference that is made available as streaming video or audio over the Web.

Window

The graphical representation of a particular file, folder or application when it is active on the Windows desktop.

Windows

A popular operating system for PC-based computers, produced by Microsoft. Different versions of Windows include Windows 3.1, Windows 95 and Windows 98.

Wizard

In Windows, a program that guides you through a complex process. Internet Explorer uses a Wizard to help you export folders of Favorites for another user to receive.

World Wide Web (WWW, or the Web)

An enormous array of linked hypertext documents that reside on computers around the world, all of which can be viewed using a browser application such as Internet Explorer.

Y

Yahoo

A popular commercial search engine.

Index